Grandma's Best Recipes

Compiled by Sarah Rodefeld

Bellissima Publishing, LLC
Jamul, California
www.bellissimapublishing.com

Copyright © 2020 by Bellissima Publishing, LLC

Front Cover, back cover and interior photos provided by Sarah Rodefeld

All rights reserved. No part of this book may be reproduced or transmitted in any form or by any means, electronic or mechanical, including any photocopying, or recording, or by any information or storage retrieval system, without permission from the
publisher and author.

ISBN 978-1-61477-466-2

First Edition

"Whether therefore ye eat, or drink, or whatsoever ye do, do all to the glory of God."

1 Corinthians 10:3,1, The Holy Bible, King James Version

Jesu Nahm govita borsh Eta drecka pok a sord Guta lella aus to god Sa fo be nata Jesu Nahm

Introduction

In today's modern world, we're all spoiled with instant gratification. The Internet, cell phones, Wi-Fi, email and video chats provide us with many avenues to get what we need and get it fast. Those cravings for mom's apple pie or Grandma's famous chocolate ice cream topping can be gotten in a mere phone call or email. If we see something on television, in a magazine or in a picture, we can hop on the Internet and get any one of a hundred recipes for it. If we don't feel like cooking, we can run to our favorite restaurant or order take-out. We're definitely blessed with a much easier life than that of the previous generations.

Back in Grandma Dorothy's day, life was much more limited and required people to be creative. The lack of money, the Great Depression and WWII all had impacts on daily life. Many meals revolved around the backyard garden or what limited items could be gotten at the small markets down the street. The literal term of "borrowing a cup of sugar" was *actually* common, and something that connected neighbors. Meals were home cooked and were eaten together at the family's table - a wholesome life in more ways than one.

Grandma Dorothy and most of the Anderson girls were children of the Great Depression. From Great-Grandma Selma and Great-Grandpa John, they learned to live within their means. Basic skills such as cooking, sewing, and gardening were taught early, and all had a part in daily life. For many of us, myself included, if we were asked to bake a homemade loaf of bread, we'd give you a blank, panicked look. For Great-Grandma Selma, she could whip up the best bread in no time flat. I have fond memories of going with Grandma Dorothy to her house and enjoying a piece of her famous freshly baked bread and butter. I've tried to reproduce her recipe and failed miserably every time. She just had that special touch.

In 1942, Grandma married her true love, Grandpa Art. Shortly after, he was sent to war and served in the Air Force in the European Theatre and ultimately became a prisoner of war. The worry was a daily thought in Grandma's mind; but with the arrival of their first son, Al, her time quickly turned from war bride, to wife and mother. That was just the start of her adventurous life!

Grandpa Art returned safely from the war and prison camp, and Art and Dorothy made their home in Rhinelander, a small town in Northern Wisconsin. Shortly after Art's return, they welcomed Sharon into the family. For many summers, Art, Dorothy, Al and Sharon spent their summers working with Art's family at the Limberlost Resort, where they made *many* friends.

Sadly, the Limberlost burned down in 1951; and Art began working in the paper industry, a career that eventually pulled them away from Rhinelander, first to Longview, Washington, then to Varadero, Cuba, and then to Augusta, Georgia. In Longview, the family lived a farming life, and the kids grew up surrounded by many friends, as well as farm animals. Many of Grandma's best recipes, and some great family stories, come from friends in Longview. As a huge animal fan, I've always enjoyed tales of the kids and their chickens, and the stories of my father, Al's, time working with the cows at the neighbor's ranch. Also during this time, Jeff was born, making their family complete. After Grandpa Art retired, he and Dorothy returned to Longview to visit friends. Their last visit was shortly after Mount St. Helens erupted. Although I was only nine, I remember quite fondly one gift they gave me from that trip -- a Kentucky Fried Chicken carton of ash they scooped up themselves from the side of the road! For a nine-year-old, that was the best gift!

While still working in the paper industry, their next stop from Longview, was a long trip to Varadero, Cuba. During their stay in Cuba, they experienced the culture and life of Caribbean living. From scuba diving, horseback riding on the beach, fishing and gatherings at the beach with friends, Art, Dorothy, Dorothy's sister, Violet, and the kids experienced *authentic* Cuba. However, during this time, the transition from Batista to Fidel Castro took place; and to ensure the family's safety, Dorothy and the family came back to Rhinelander, while Art remained in Cuba to pack things up. Art then transitioned to Puerto Rico for a short period of time before returning to Rhinelander. Art then accepted a position at a paper plant in Georgia and so the family moved to Augusta, Georgia. After a year in Augusta, they realized Southern life was not for them!

Al and the family dog were the first to return back to Rhinelander; and they were quickly followed by the rest of the family. Rhinelander was now, and always will be, home!

Art's family, Josie and Ed, ran the Oaken Bucket Cottages on the beautiful shore of Thunder Lake. As time went on, and after Ed passed away, Josie turned the cottages over to Art and his sister, Jen. Art eventually bought out Jen, making them owners of their own resort. For the rest of their lives, they spent summers hosting a multitude of generations of guests who ultimately turned into life-long friends. Many meals, stories, parties and fishing trips full of grandiose stories were shared over the years and still are to this day.

Art and Dorothy were also members of Immanuel Lutheran Church. Dorothy was active in many of the church's Circles and offered her sewing talents making blankets for the church's relief efforts. The Swedish heritage of both her and Art provided Dorothy with the skills needed to cook Lefse and other Swedish specialties for the church's socials and fund raising. Immanuel was blessed with the best cooks Rhinelander had to offer, and through church gatherings and their numerous cookbooks, our family had access to many tasty meals.

The Anderson sisters, Dorothy, Lorriane, Linnette, Margaret, Violet, Janice and Sandy all remained close. Except for Lorraine and Sandy, they all lived in Rhinelander. Sadly, Great-Grandpa John passed away years before Selma. After his death, all of the sisters made sure Great-Grandma was very well taken care of until her death. For many years, the Anderson girls and their families gathered at Christmas to celebrate the Holiday season, sharing stories and enjoying the many, many wonderful recipes that each of the seven sisters shared with one another. And Grandma Dorothy always made sure Great-Grandma Selma had her traditional Lutefisk dinner at Christmas. (Most of us learned that this was a meal *only* for the *stout Swedish members* of the family, and we quickly cleared out until the smell of that meal was gone.)

Even as time went on, and Dorothy and Art had steady income from Art's retirement and the resort, Dorothy often fell back to sharing the simple meals that were cooked during the war. Grandpa's very favorite was Velling, a milk soup with basic dumplings made from the broth and flour. (It was very good; but sadly, I never did manage to get Grandma to write it down for future generations. Recipes are on the web for it, but they don't match with my recollections of her simplified recipe. Maybe someday I'll figure that one out.)

In each place they lived, they were welcomed warmly by new friends and neighbors. The sharing of meals and recipes was the "Internet of their day." Many of our favorite family meals have come directly from these travels. While some meals, like the Cuban tradition of cooking pigs in a pit, were not one regularly, their Cuban friends *did* make it to Rhinelander to share that tradition again with our entire family.

As I learned to cook, I would always get frustrated as I watched my grandmothers make these wonderful meals It was always "just a pinch pinch of this", or a good dollop of that". I needed things in a measurable amount, but that's how that generation worked. I remember fondly the last time I cooked with my other Grandma, Grandma Florence. We were making her famous donuts. As she went through the recipe, she would cut off ¾ stick of butter, but the !recipe called for 2 TBSP. Big difference – but those donuts turned out perfectly! And if I hadn't watched her, and made notes on my copy, all would have been lost with that favorite recipe! And so I vowed I would never do any of that. Well, as I get older, and go to share a few of my own recipes, I realize I do the very same thing! I've turned into my grandmothers, and I'm so grateful for that! It's made me a better cook. The old ways are truly timeless.

As I cook Grandma Dorothy's recipes for my family, I hope she knew how much we appreciated all the time and effort she put in to making life so special for all of us. She once told me how lucky she was to have all of us; but I can honestly say that from all the customized birthday cakes she made for us grandkids, to the endless Christmas cookies and goodies, to the many times she fried fish for all of us gluttons, not eating hers until the family had their fill – we were definitely the lucky ones.

I hope you enjoy these family recipes. And as a suggestion...unless you're a stout Swedish fisherman, I would stay away from the Lutefisk!

Sarah

Grandma's Best Recipes

As Compiled by Sarah Rodefeld

Table of Recipes, Etc.

Sweets and Deserts 3

Dips and Snacks 55

Breads, Pancakes, Etc. 61

Side Dishes 83

A Quick Note From The Chef 113

Main Dishes 115

Miscellaneous 137

Soups 161

Seabloom Family Mealtime Prayers . . . 171

About the Author 172

Grandma's Best Recipes

The Seabloom Family Cookbook

I have gathered all the recipes that were in Grandma Dorothy's recipe boxes that she collected through the years. Many not only came from Grandma, but also came from other members of Grandma and Grandpa's extended families. Great Grandma Selma Anderson and Great-Aunt Violet, Great Aunt Nettie, Great Aunt Margaret, Great Aunt Lorraine, and reat Aunt Janice all had great recipes that are included in this book! I did my best to include all the recipes that I know we have always either loved or enjoyed or have had some good laughs over. You may find variations of some recipes, with different ingredients and/or cooking methods. I hope you enjoy the recipes as much as I enjoyed putting this together. Grandma has kept a lot of neat things in her recipe cookbooks books and recipe boxes, and it was fun to find and read her notes.

- *Sarah* -

Grandma's Best Recipes

"Bless O Lord this food to use and us to thy service and make us ever mindful of the needs of others. In Jesus name – Amen"

Grandma's Best Recipes

Sweets & Desserts

Grandma's Best Recipes

And out of the ground made the Lord God to grow every tree that is pleasant to the sight, and good for food; the tree of life also in the midst of the garden, and the tree of knowledge of good and evil.

Genesis 2:9   The Holy Bible, King James Version

Grandma's Best Recipes

Sweets & Desserts

Date Balls
1 pound dates
2 cups sugar
1 cup butter

Cook until thick. Add six cups Rice Krispies and make into balls. Roll in nuts or coconu

Gingerbread (second cousin Penny)
½ cup sugar
½ cup oil
2 eggs
1 cup dark molasses
2 ½ cups all purpose flour
2 tsp baking soda
1 tsp cinnamon
1 tsp ginger
½ tsp ground cloves
½ tsp salt
1 cup of hot water

Mix in order given. Preheat oven to 350 degrees. Liberally spray a 9 inch square pan with cooking spray. Pour batter into pan and bake in preheated oven until knife in center comes out clean. Serve with canned whipped cream.

Grandma's Best Recipes

Caramels (from Jeano)
1 Cup butter
1 pound Brown Sugar
Dash Salt
1 Cup light corn syrup
1 15 oz. can sweetened condensed milk
1 tsp vanilla

Melt butter in 3 qt. saucepan. Add brown sugar and salt. Stir until thoroughly combined. Blend in corn syrup. Gradually add milk stirring constantly. Cook and stir over medium heat until candy reaches 245 degrees. Remove from heat and stir in vanilla. Pour into buttered 9x9 pan. Cool thoroughly. Cut into squares and wrap. Don't scrape pan.

Fudge
4 ½ cups sugar
1 can evaporated milk
¼ pound butter
Boil five minutes
Add:
4 pkgs. chocolate chips
1 pint marshmallow crème
Vanilla and nuts
Makes about five pounds.

Grandma's Best Recipes

Oatmeal Cookies
1 cup shortening
1 cup granulated sugar
1 cup firmly packed brown sugar
2 eggs
1 tsp vanilla
1 cup sifted all-purpose flour
1 tsp baking powder
½ tsp salt
1 tsp cinnamon
¼ tsp nutmeg
1 cups quick Buckeye Rolled Oats uncooked

Heat oven to moderate 350 degrees. Place shortening, sugars, eggs and vanilla in mixing bowl. Beat thoroughly. Sift together flour, baking powder, salt, cinnamon and nutmeg. Add to shortening mixture. Mix thoroughly. Stir in oats. Drop from teaspoon onto greased cookie sheets. Bake in preheated oven 12-15 minutes. For variety, add chopped nuts, raisins, chocolate chips, dates or coconut to the dough.

Butter Cookies
1 ½ cups butter (3/4 pound)
1 1/3 cups sugar
1 tsp baking powder
1 tbsp. vanilla
2 eggs
4 cups flour

Cream butter and sugar; add eggs and vanilla. Add flour and baking powder. Roll out and cut with cookie cutters. Bake at 350 degrees for ten minutes or until done. Chill dough before rolling out.

Grandma's Best Recipes

Carmel Frosting
1 ½ cup brown sugar
1/3 cup cream
Butter
Vanilla
Cool and add powdered sugar.
2 ½ cups confectioners' sugar

Mocha Frosting
2 tbsp. cream
2 tbsp. oleo
½ cup cocoa
4 tbsp. strong coffee
Vanilla
Pinch of salt

Grandma's Best Recipes

Grandma's Almond Rolls with Icing
4 cups flour
4 tbsp. sugar
1 cup butter or oleo
1 tsp salt
1 cup warm milk
1/3 large yeast or 2 packages dry yeast
2 eggs beaten

Sift dry ingredients – work in butter like piecrust. Beat eggs, soften yeast in warm milk. Pour in liquid and work into a ball. Refrigerate overnight. Divide into three balls. Roll each ball into a circle. Spread with your choice of almond or poppy seed spread. Cut into wedge. Roll from wide end to point. Let rise till doubled. Brush with melted butter. Bake in moderate oven 10-12 minutes. Frost with powder sugar icing.

Pistachio Dessert
Crust:
48 Ritz crackers crushed
1 stick oleo melted
Mix and put in 9x12 pan. Bake for 10 minutes at 350 degrees.
Filling:
2 Packages instant (Royal) Pistachio pudding
1 ½ cups cold milk
1 Quart vanilla ice cream

Mix and put on cooled crust. Refrigerate 30 minutes. Top with cool whip, chopped nuts, and 2 grated Heath candy bars. Refrigerate.

Grandma's Best Recipes

Date or Prune Bars
¾ cup shortening
1 cup brown sugar
1 ¾ cups flour
½ tsp soda
1 tsp salt
1 ½ cup oatmeal
3 cups dates or prunes
¼ cup sugar
1 ½ cups water

Bake at 400 degrees for 25-30 minutes. Add orange juice if prunes are used.

Mounds Bars
1 ½ cup graham cracker crumbs
1/3 cup sugar
½ cup butter, melted
1 ½ cup flaked coconut
1 can sweetened condensed milk (14 oz.)
1 cup real chocolate chip morsels melted

Preheat oven to 350 degrees. Mix cracker crumbs, sugar and butter in bowl. Pat into 13x9 ungreased pan. Bake 10 minutes. Mix coconut and condensed milk. Spoon onto hot crust. Bake 15 minutes. Cool ten minutes. Spoon chocolate evenly over warm cake. Cook until chocolate sets. Cut into small squares. Makes about 40 squares.

Grandma's Best Recipes

White Cake
½ cup butter (creamed)
Sift 1 ½ cups sugar and add gradually
1 cup water
3 cups flour – sifted once. Measure and sift 3 times and add 3 tsp baking powder, 4 egg whites, salt and one tsp vanilla. No baking directions were noted.

Crustless Pumpkin Torte
1 large can pumpkin
6 eggs
1 can evaporated milk
1 ¾ cups sugar
1 tsp vanilla
2 tsp cinnamon
1 tsp ginger
½ tsp cloves
½ tsp salt

Beat all together to blend and pour into greased 9x13 pan. Cut ½ stick oleo into 1 pkg. white or yellow Jiffy cake mix and sprinkle over top. Bake at 350 for one hour. Top with Cool Whip.

Grandma's Best Recipes

Angel Food Candy
2 cups light brown sugar
2 cups light corn syrup
4 tsp. baking soda

Combine sugar and syrup in a 3-quart saucepan. Cook to 290 degrees. Use a candy thermometer. Remove from heat. Add baking soda. Beat very quickly until well blended. It will foam up. Pour into a battered 15 ½ x 10 ½ inch pan. Let cool. Break mixture into pieces after hardened. You can dip into chocolate or you can melt a block of milk chocolate and drizzle over the mixture. If the chocolate becomes cake-like, just add a teaspoon or so of buttery Crisco until it is thin again.

Homemade Chocolates
Mix by hand, 2 pounds powdered sugar, one can Eagle Brand condensed sweetened milk, two sticks oleo and 1 tsp vanilla. Roll in balls and freeze. You can use various additions such as coconut, cherries etc. Melt 1 pound chocolate chips and 1 pound butterscotch chips in top of double boiler. Add ½ cup paraffin – dip the frozen candies in hot chocolate mixture.

Pecan Puffs
1 cup butter
4 tbsp. sugar
¼ tsp salt
2 cups cake flour
2 cups pecans

Bake at 300 degrees for 45 minutes. Roll in powdered sugar.

Grandma's Best Recipes

Angel Food Cake
1 1/8 cups sifted flour (1 cup plus 2 tbsp.)
¾ cup sugar
Sift above ingredients together.
In a large bowl:
Beat 1 ½ cups egg whites
½ tsp salt

Beat on number 10 speed until foamy. Add 1 ½ tsp cream of tartar and continue on number 10 speed until whites are stiff and in peaks. Do not overbeat. Add 1 cup sifted sugar and continue on number 8 speed till sugar is blended. Turn to number 2 speed and add 1 tsp vanilla, 1 tsp. almond, and sprinkle in sifted flour evenly and quickly. Beat only to blend. Bake 375 degrees for 35 minutes.

Mandarin Orange Cake
1 yellow cake mix (follow package directions)
1 can mandarin oranges, fold into batter (Juice and all)
Bake according to directions
Frosting:
1 15 oz. can crushed pineapple (juice and all)
1 box instant vanilla pudding
Mix together then fold in one small cool whip.

Grandma's Best Recipes

Fattigman – Grandma's Christmas Tradition
3 eggs yolks
1 egg
4 tbsp. sugar
3 tbsp. real cream or melted butter
Almond extract
Pinch of salt
Flour to make a stiff dough.

Roll thin and cut into shapes and fry in deep fat. Aunt Jane used lard. Sprinkle with powdered sugar.

Frosting for Brownies
1 cup powdered sugar
1 tbsp. cocoa
2 tbsp. butter
2 tbsp. cream
Cook until it boils on sides of pan. Remove and beat until right consistency. Cut while frosting is still warm.

Grandma's Best Recipes

Rhubarb Strawberry Pie
1 cup sugar
5 tbsp. sugar
Mix together:
Two cups rhubarb and strawberries. Mix with sugar and flour. Dot with butter. Bake at 425 degrees for 40 minutes. Use more sugar if you use fresh strawberries.

Baked Rhubarb Dessert
1 cup flour
1 ½ tsp baking powder
2 tbsp. sugar
1 tbsp. butter
1 egg beaten
2 tbsp. milk

Make batter by adding egg, milk, and butter to sifted dry ingredients. Press into 9x9 inch pan. Spread filling over batter.

Filling:
3 cups diced rhubarb
1 package strawberry Jell-O
1/3 cup sugar
2 tbsp. flour
Mix and spread over batter. Add topping.
Topping:
1 cup sugar
½ cup flour
¼ cup butter
Combine and spread over filling. Bake ½ hour at 375 degrees. Top with cream or ice cream. May be reheated.

Grandma's Best Recipes

Molasses Cookies
5 cups flour
1 tsp cream of tartar
1 tsp baking soda
1 tsp ginger
½ tsp cinnamon
½ tsp salt
1 cup packed brown sugar
1 cup butter or oleo
3 eggs
1 cup light molasses
¼ cup buttermilk
Roll out – sprinkle with sugar. Bake at 375 degrees for 8-15 minutes.

Banana Bread (Selma Anderson)
1 cup sugar
2 eggs
½ cup canola oil
½ tsp salt
3 mashed bananas
2 cups flour
1 tsp soda
Walnuts (optional)

Mix all together. Bake at 350 degrees until done.

Grandma's Best Recipes

Sour Cream Coffee Cake
2 cups flour
1 tsp baking powder
1 tsp soda
½ tsp salt
½ cup butter or oleo
1 cup sugar
2 eggs
1 cup sour cream
1 tsp vanilla
Topping:
2 tbsp. butter or oleo
2 tbsp. sugar
¼ cup fine bread crumbs
¼ cups flour
1 ½ tsp cinnamon
¼ cup chopped nuts

Preheat oven to 350 degrees. Grease 13x9x2 pan. Sift together flour baking powder soda and salt. Cream oleo adding sugar until light and fluffy. Add eggs one at a time creaming well after each added item. Add dry ingredients with sour cream beating well. Add vanilla. Turn batter into prepared pan. Sprinkle streusel evenly over top. Bake 35-40 minutes or until done. Topping: cream butter and sugar add bread crumbs, flour and cream to consistency of course crumbs. Mix in nuts.

Grandma's Best Recipes

Date and Ritz Crackers
50 Ritz crackers
1 can sweetened condensed milk
8 oz. dates
½ cup nuts (more or less)

Combine milk, dates and nuts. Cook over hot water until thick. Add vanilla and put 1 tsp. filling on each cracker. Bake 8 minutes at 350 degrees.
Frosting – 2 cups powdered sugar, 4 oz. cream cheese, vanilla and milk to thin.

Foolproof Fudge
3 – 6 oz. package chocolate chips
1 can sweetened condensed milk
Dash of salt
1 ½ tsp vanilla
½ cup nuts

In heavy sauce pan, over low heat, melt chocolate chips with Eagle brand milk. Remove from heat and stir in remaining ingredients. Put in 8-inch pan lined with wax paper. Chill until firm. Turn onto board and cut into squares.

Grandma's Best Recipes

Nutty Cookie Crust
Use pie pan
½ cup soft butter or margarine
¼ cup sifted confectioner's sugar
½ tsp vanilla
1 cup flour
1/8 tsp salt
½ cup nuts

Mix butter, sugar and vanilla thoroughly. Stir flour and salt together. Add to mixture and blend. Add chopped nuts (optional). Chill 30-45 minutes. Heat oven to 400 degrees. Pat dough evenly into ungreased pie pan. Bake 10-12 minutes or until lightly browned. Cool. Fill with ice cream.

No Crust Coconut Custard Pie
2 cups milk
4 eggs
6 tbsp. soft butter or oleo
2/3 cup sugar
Dash of salt
½ cup flour
½ tsp nutmeg
1 tsp vanilla
1 cup flaked coconut

Heat oven to 325 degrees. Grease and flour 9-inch glass pie pan. Put all ingredients in a blender and blend well for one minute. Pour into greased pie pan. Bake at 325 degrees for 50 minutes or until knife inserted in center comes out clean. Pie forms its own crust.

Grandma's Best Recipes

Peanut Butter Burst Pan Cookies
2 cups flour
1 tsp baking powder
¼ tsp salt
1 cup butter softened
¾ cup brown sugar firmly packed
½ cup sugar
½ tsp vanilla
1 egg
12 ounces of peanut butter morsels

Bake at 375 degrees for 20-25 minutes in a 15x10x1 pan.

Cheerios Nuggets
1 cup packed brown sugar
½ cup margarine or butter, softened
¼ cup light corn syrup
½ tsp salt
¼ tsp baking soda
6 cups Cheerios cereal
1 cup salted peanuts
1 cup raisins

Heat oven to 250 degrees. Grease two 13x9x2 pans or one jellyroll pan that is 15 ½ x 10 ½ x 1 inch. Heat brown sugar, oleo, corn syrup and salt in 2-quart saucepan over medium heat, stirring constantly until bubbly around edges. Cook uncovered stirring occasionally, two minutes longer. Remove from heat and stir in baking soda until foamy and lightly colored. Pour over cereal, peanuts and raisins in greased 4-quart bowl. Stir until mixture is coated. Spread evenly in pan. Bake 15 minutes. Stir and let stand just until cool – about ten minutes. Loosen mixture with metal spatula. Let stand until firm – about 30 minutes. Break into bite-sized pieces. About 10 cups of snacks.

Grandma's Best Recipes

Marshmallow Cream Fudge Peanut Butter
2 c white sugar
2/3 cup can milk
Put together and boil to soft stage (238 degrees – Rolling Boil for five minutes)
Add:
1 stick oleo
1 cup peanut butter
1 cup marshmallow cream
1 tsp vanilla
Stir until combined. Pour in small square cake pan.

Jeano's Dessert
1 large and 1 small container Cool Whip
5 separated eggs
3 tbsp. sugar
1 angel food cake
1 cup broken nuts
2 small or 1 large chips

Melt chips and 3 tbsp. water. Add yolks beaten with sugar. Beat egg whites stiff and fold into above mixture. Add cool whip and nuts. Break ½ cake into small pieces into bottom of pan and add ½ mixture. Repeat with second half.

Grandma's Best Recipes

Grandma's Christmas Sugar Cookies
1 Cup sugar
2 sticks oleo
2 eggs
3 cups flour
1 tsp vanilla
1 tsp soda
1 tsp cream of tartar
¼ tsp salt

Roll out and cut with cutters. Bake at 350 degrees for 7-10 minutes.

Norwegian Toast
1 ½ cup sugar
1 cup butter
Cream above together.
Add two eggs and beat
Stir in 1 cup sour cream
½ tsp salt
1 tsp cardamom
1 tsp mace
1 tsp soda

Beat all above until smooth. Divide batter on large cookie sheet. Make 2 flat cakes. Use spoon - they should be 1 ½ inch high. Bake for 20 minutes at 375 degrees or until done. Remove and slice while hot. Place on sheets and bake for 20 minutes at 375 degrees.

Grandma's Best Recipes

Rice Krispie Bars
¼ cup butter
40 marshmallows or 4 cups mini marshmallows
5 cups Rice Krispies

Melt butter. Add marshmallows and mix continuously. Add rice krispies. Pour into a 9x13 greased pan.

Anise Candy
4 cups sugar
2 cups white syrup
¾ cup water

Boil until hard ball stage. Add any vegetable coloring and small amount of anise flavoring – about 2 ½ tsp.

Cranberry Apple Cake
1 ¼ cup sugar
½ cup oil
Mix well.
Add:
2 eggs
1 tsp soda
1 tsp salt
1 tsp vanilla
2 cups flour
Add:
2 cups finely sliced apples
½ pound whole cranberries
½ cup nuts

Bake in a 9x13 pan for 40-50 minutes. (oven temperature not given)

Grandma's Best Recipes

Peanut Butter Chocolate Chip Cookies
1 cup shortening
1 cup brown sugar
1 cup sugar
1 tsp vanilla
2 eggs, beaten
1 cup peanut butter
3 cups sifted flour
2 tsp soda
Dash salt
1 cup chopped nuts
2 cups chocolate chips

Cream shortening, sugars and vanilla. Add eggs, beat thoroughly. Stir in peanut butter. Sift dry ingredients and stir into creamed mixture. Add chips and nuts. Drop by spoonfuls onto greased

Pecan Pie (Jeano Seabloom)
¼ cup butter or oleo
1 cup brown sugar
1 cup Karo syrup (dark or light)
¼ tsp salt
1 tsp vanilla
3 eggs well beaten
1 cup pecan halves

Cream sugar and oleo. Add syrup, salt and vanilla. Add eggs – beat well. Add pecans. Bake 350 degrees for 50 minutes.

Raspberry Pie
To one box of frozen berries add 1 cup sugar, ¾ cup water, and 2 tbsp. cornstarch. Cook until thick. Pour into baked pie shell and serve with whipped cream.

Grandma's Best Recipes

Molasses Cake
1 cup sugar
Tbsp. butter
2 eggs
1 cup sour milk
1 tsp soda
½ cup molasses
Flour (amount not listed)
1 tsp baking powder
1 tsp cinnamon

Bake 375 for 10 minutes.

Grandma's Famous Chocolate Sauce (like hot fudge)
¾ cup chocolate chips
2 cups powdered sugar
1 stick oleo
1 ½ cup evaporated milk (one can)
1 tsp vanilla

Melt chocolate chips and oleo. Add sugar and milk. Cook 8 minutes and add vanilla. Cook ten minutes more.

Krumkake
¾ cup butter
1 cup sugar
4 eggs
1 1/3 cups sifted all-purpose flour
2/3 cup corn starch
1 tsp vanilla (the recipe originally said cardamom but Grandma crossed it out and added vanilla)

Cream butter and sugar, beaten eggs, and dry ingredients. Drop by teaspoon on Krumkake iron. Makes 4-5 dozen.

Grandma's Best Recipes

Pumpkin Pie
1 cup cooked pumpkin
2 eggs
1/3 cup sugar
1 cup milk
½ tsp salt
½ tsp ginger
¼ tsp cinnamon

Heat milk. Add pumpkin. Beat eggs and add spices and sugar, etc. Bake custard until done - 450 degrees for ten minutes. Reduce heat to 350 and finish baking.

Apple or Cherry Cake
2 eggs, beaten
1 cup sugar
1 cup flour
2 cups apples – diced
1 ½ tsp. baking powder
Dash of salt

Topping:
1/3 cup sugar or more
2/3 cup flour
6 tbsp. butter
1 tsp cinnamon

Bake in 13x9x2 pan for 45 minutes at 350 degrees. Drizzle with frosting – ½ cup powdered sugar – milk and vanilla – thin.

Grandma's Best Recipes

Apple Crisp
6 large apples
1 tsp Cinnamon
1 cup water
7 tbsp. butter – melted
1 cup sugar
¾ cup flour

Slice apples in baking dish. Mix cinnamon into apples. Pour cup of water over. Mix together butter, flour and sugar. Press on top of apples. Bake until tender.

French Pastry Bars
Work together the following:
1 cup flour
½ cup butter
¼ cup brown sugar
Pat in 7x13 pan and bake in 350 degree for 10 minutes.
Mix the following together:
2 beaten eggs
2 tbsp. flour
1 tsp baking powder
1 ½ cup brown sugar
1 cup chopped nuts
½ cup coconut
1 tsp vanilla

Spread over baked layer in cookie pan. Bake for 20 minutes. Cut into squares. Dust with powdered sugar and store in refrigerator.

Grandma's Best Recipes

Chocolate Syrup Brownies
1 stick oleo
1 cup sugar
4 eggs
1 cup plus 2 tbsp. flour
½ tsp salt
1-16 oz. can chocolate syrup
Beat first five ingredients. Add syrup last. Bake 350 for 30 minutes.
Frosting:
1 ½ cup sugar
6 tbsp. canned milk
6 tbsp. oleo
½ cup chips

Bring to rolling boil for three minutes. Add chocolate chips and beat. Frost brownies.

Fudge Krispies
One 11 ½ oz. (2 cups) milk chocolate morsels
½ cup oleo
½ cup light corn syrup
2 tsp Vanilla
1 cup sifted confectioners sugar
4 cups Kellog's Rice Krispies

Combine milk chocolate morsels, oleo and corn syrup in sauce pan. Stir over low heat until melted and smooth. Remove from heat. Stir in vanilla and sugar. Add Rice Krispies mixing lightly until well coated. Spread evenly in 13x9 pan. Chill until firm. Cut into squares. Store in refrigerator.

Grandma's Best Recipes

Chocolate Crispy Cookies
2 ½ cups un-sifted all-purpose flour
1 tsp soda
½ tsp salt
1 cup oleo
2 cups sugar
2 eggs
2 tsp vanilla
4 cups rice krispies cereal
1 12 oz. semi-sweet chocolate chips

Preheat oven to 350 degrees. Stir together flour, soda, and salt. Set aside. Beat oleo and sugar until smooth. Beat in eggs and vanilla. Mix in flour mixture. Gradually stir in rice krispies and semi-sweet chips. Drop by level measuring tbsp. onto greased baking sheet. Bake 350 degrees for about 10 minutes or until lightly browned. Makes 7 doz.

Criss Crosses
1 cup shortening
1 tsp vanilla
1 cup granulated sugar
1 cup brown sugar
2 beaten eggs
1 cup peanut butter
3 cups flour
1/8 tsp salt
2 tsp soda

Form in small balls and press with a fork. Bake 375 degrees for 10 minutes.

Grandma's Best Recipes

Swedish Ginger Cookies
1 cup shortening
1 cup sugar
1 cup dark molasses
1 tsp ginger
1 tsp cinnamon
1 tsp nutmeg
Blend and bring to a boil. <u>Cool</u>. Add 2 eggs (beaten) mix well.
Sift together:
5 cups flour
1 tsp baking powder
1 tsp baking soda
1 tsp salt
Add dry ingredients and chill.

Roll 1/8 inch thick – Bake 10-12 minutes at 350-375 degrees.

Lemon Whippersnaps
1 Package Pillsbury Lemon Cake Mix
2 cups (4½ oz.) frozen whipped topping
1 egg
½ cup sifted powdered sugar

Grease cookie sheet. Combine cake mix, whipped topping and 1 egg in large bowl. Stir until well mixed. Drop by tsp into powdered sugar mixture. Roll until coated. Place 1 ½ inches apart on cookie sheet. Bake 350 degrees for 10-15 minutes until light golden brown. Remove from cookie sheet. Cool. Makes 4 dozen cookies.

Grandma's Best Recipes

Graham Cracker Cookies
1 cup brown sugar – firmly packed
1 cup butter
1 cup nuts

Melt butter and add brown sugar. Boil 2 minutes and add nuts. In 10x15 pan, lay graham crackers so lines on crackers are the same. Pour above ingredients over the top. Bake ten minutes at 350 degrees. Cook for 5-10 minutes. Cut and separate.

Hard Cooked Egg Yolk Cookies
2 hard cooked egg yolks – mashed
¼ cup sugar
½ cup butter
1 cup flour
Almond flavoring to taste.

Bake 12 minutes at 325 degrees

Grandma's Best Recipes

The Favorite Christmas Carmel Corn
2 cups light brown sugar firmly packed
½ cup light corn syrup
½ pound oleo
¼ tsp. cream of tartar
1 tsp. salt
1 tsp. baking soda
6 quarts popped corn

In 2 ½ quart saucepan – combine brown sugar, corn syrup, butter, cream of tartar and salt. Bring to boil, stirring over medium high heat. Stir constantly. Bring to a boil rapidly to hard ball stage 260 degrees (about five minutes) Remove from heat. Stir in baking soda quickly but thoroughly. Pour at once over popcorn in large long pan all laid out. Mix gently until all kernels are coated. Bake at 200 degrees for one hour. Stir two or three times during baking. Turn out at once on wax paper. Spread and allow to cool completely. Break apart and store in a tightly covered container. Makes six quarts.

Cream Cheese Cookies
½ cup shortening
3 oz. cream cheese
¼ cup sugar
½ tsp vanilla
1 cup flour

Cream shortening, cheese, sugar and vanilla. Blend in flour – Put through press. Bake 8-10 minutes at 375 degrees.

Grandma's Best Recipes

Orange Cake (Nettie Anderson Musson)
1 cup sugar
½ cup butter
1 cup sour cream
2 eggs
¼ tsp salt
1 tsp soda
1 tsp baking powder
1 tsp vanilla
2 cups flour

Grind one orange, one cup raisins, ¼ cup chopped nuts. Save 1/3 for topping. Bake 350 degrees for 35 minutes.

Lemon Cheese Bars
1 package yellow cake mix with pudding
1/3 cup sugar
1 tsp lemon juice
8 oz. cream cheese – softened
1/3 cup oil
2 eggs

Mix dry cake mix one egg and oil until crumbly. Reserve 1 cup. Press remaining crumbs lightly in an ungreased 9x13x2 pan. Bake 15 minutes at 350 degrees. Beat cheese, lemon juice and one egg until light and smooth. Spread over baked layer. Sprinkle with reserved crumb mixture. Bake 15 minutes longer. Cool. Cut into bars.

Grandma's Best Recipes

Peanut Butter Cups (no cook)
2 cups peanut butter
2 cups powdered sugar
2 cups graham cracker crumbs

Mix together and roll in balls. Dunk in melted chocolate or Press firmly in small pan and spread melted chocolate over the top.

Apple Crisp
6 large apples, peeled and cored
1 tsp cinnamon
1 cup water
7 tablespoons melted butter
1 cup sugar
¾ cup flour

Slice apples into baking dish. Mix cinnamon in with apples. Pour the cup of water over the apples. Mix together the butter, flour and sugar. Press on top of apples. Bake at 350 degrees until tender.

Grandma's Best Recipes

Bread Pudding
6 cups milk
12 cups day old bread cut into two-inch cubes
¾ cup melted butter
1 ½ cups sugar
6 eggs slightly beaten
¾ tsp salt
1 ½ cup raisins
3 tsp cinnamon
Dash of nutmeg
Sauce:
2 cups sugar
1 cup butter
1 ½ cup half and half

Pudding: Scald milk and then pour over bread. Let set until cool. When cooled, add butter, sugar, eggs, salt, raisins, cinnamon and nutmeg. Mix and pour into greased 9x13 pan. Bake at 375 degrees for one hour and 15 minutes or until knife inserted in center comes out clean. Serve with Sauce.

Sauce: Cook the sugar, butter and half and half in double boiler until sugar is dissolved and sauce is smooth. Pour over pudding and serve hot.

Grandma's Best Recipes

Buttery Peanut Brittle
2 cups white sugar
1 cup light corn syrup
½ cup water
1 cup butter or margarine
1 cup raw Spanish peanuts
1 tsp baking soda
Candy Thermometer
5 or 6 9-inch aluminum pie pans

Butter top 1 inch of heavy three quart saucepan. Combine sugar, syrup and water. Cook and stir until sugar dissolves. Bring to boiling; blend in butter. Stir frequently after mixture reaches 230 degrees. Add nuts when temperature is at 280 degrees (soft crack stage), stir constantly until mixture reaches hard crack stage (305 degrees). Remove from heat; quickly stir in soda, mixing thoroughly. It will almost bubble over top of pan. Pour into buttered pie pans. Place on cooling rack. Let sit until cool (about 10 minutes) and pop out of pans.

Divinity
2 ½ cups sugar
½ cup white Karo Syrup
1 cup hot water
2 egg whites
½ tsp vanilla
½ tsp almond
(if almond is not used, use 1 tsp vanilla)
Nutmeats

Boil sugar, syrup and water to 243 degrees. Then beat egg whites very stiff. Pour syrup in slowly – continue beating until it holds its shape when dropped from a spoon. Add flavoring (nut meats optional). Drop by teaspoon on waxed paper.

Grandma's Best Recipes

Topping for German Chocolate Cake
2/3 cup sugar
2/3 cup evaporated milk
2 egg yolks
1/3 cup shortening
½ tsp vanilla
1 1/3 cups (3 ½ oz. can) flaked coconut
1 cup chopped pecans

Combine: Sugar, milk, yolks and shortening. Let come to a boil over medium heat. Remove. Add coconut, nuts and vanilla. Let stand 15 minutes to cool.

Hot Butter Sauce
¼ cup butter
½ cups sugar
6 tbsp. milk

Boil one minute

Chocolate Glaze
In small pan bring ¼ cup sugar and ¼ cup water to a rolling boil – stirring until all sugar is dissolved. Remove from heat. Immediately add 1 cup semi-sweet chocolate chips. Stir with wire whisk until chips are all melted and smooth. Cool until slightly thickened.

Chocolate Frosting
Mix well in a heavy 1 ½ quart sauce pan – 1 pkg. chocolate pudding (not the instant kind), 1 cup sugar and ½ cup PET evaporated milk. Cook and stir to a full, all-over boil. Lower heat, stir and boil slowly for 3 minutes. Take off heat. Without stirring add 1 tbsp. butter and let cool ten minutes. Stir mixture until very thick. Add 2 tsp. evaporated milk and stir until thick enough to spread on a cooled cake.

Grandma's Best Recipes

Frosting
1 package Dream Whip
1 package instant pudding
1 ½ cup milk
Beat all together

Creamy Frosting
1 package (4 oz.) instant pudding
½ cup powdered sugar
1 8-ounce cool whip – thawed

Combine pudding mix, sugar and milk and beat slowly until well blended – about one minute. Fold in whipped topping. Spread on cake at once. Cake should be refrigerated. For firmer frosting, let mixture stand before adding cool whip.

Peanut Butter Bars
1 ½ cup graham cracker crumbs
1 1/3 stick oleo or butter
1 cup chunky peanut butter
2 cups powdered sugar

Mix together and put in a 9x13 pan. Melt 12 oz. of milk chocolate chips and spread over top. Refrigerate until chocolate is set then cut into bars. These freeze well.

Grandma's Best Recipes

S'Mores Bars
¾ cup butter melted
3 cups graham cracker crumbs
1/3 cup sugar
1 cup chocolate chips
2 cups mini marshmallows

Combine butter, crumbs and sugar. Press half firmly into greased 9x13 pan. Sprinkle chocolate chips and marshmallows and remaining crumbs. Press down. Bake at 375 for 10 minutes. Press down firmly with pancake turner. Cool completely before cutting.

Banana Split Torte
Preheat oven to 350 degrees
Crust:
2 ½ cups graham cracker crumbs
4 tbsp. sugar
½ cup melted margarine
Mix. Press mixture into a 13x9 pan. Bake for 7 minutes. Cool.
Topping:
2 sticks soft oleo or butter
2 cups powdered sugar
2 eggs

Beat about 20 minutes until mixture turns to custard. Spread over cooled crust. Layer 4-5 bananas split lengthwise over custard.
1 large can crushed pineapple, drained
1 large container cool whip

Sprinkle crushed pecans over top, if desired. Cut maraschino cherries in half and place over each piece. Drizzle Hershey chocolate syrup over top. Refrigerate overnight or six hours. Serves 15-20.

Grandma's Best Recipes

Strawberry Rhubarb Upside Down Cake
2 cups diced rhubarb
2/3 cups sugar
1 tbsp. water
1 package white cake mix (18 oz.)
3 tbsp. flour
1 package 3 oz. strawberry gelatin
1/3 cup cooking oil
4 eggs
1 cup plus 2 tbsp. water
Sweetened whipped cream

Combine rhubarb, sugar and water mixing well. Let stand about 30 minutes at room temperature. Combine cake mix, flour and gelatin mixing well. Add oil, eggs and half of water. Mix until smooth. Spread rhubarb mixture in 13x9 pan. Spoon batter over top. Bake in oven preheated to 375 degrees about 45 minutes or until wooden toothpick inserted comes out clean. Loosen side of cake with spatula. Cool in pan inverted on plate. Serve warm with cream.

Butterscotch Pie
1 cup brown sugar
2 egg yolks
2 tbsp. flour
1 cup milk
1 tbsp. butter

Mix sugar and flour and egg yolks together and stir until smooth. Add milk and cook over water until it thickens. Add butter and pour in baked pie shell. Top with meringue and brown in hot oven.

Grandma's Best Recipes

Cherry Custard Pie
Sprinkle 1 tbsp. flour and two tbsp. sugar on bottom of unbaked crust. Over this pour 2 cups sour cherries (drained cherries). Mix:
2 egg yolks
1 cup sugar
2 tbsp. flour
1 tbsp. melted butter
1 cup milk
Pour over cherries

Bake in moderate oven until custard is set. Cover with meringue.

Cherry Custard Kuchen
½ cup butter
1 cup flour
2 tbsp. sugar
Yolk of one egg
Filling:
1 ½ cans cherries (drained)

Spread on crust. Beat 2 eggs, one cup of sugar, pinch of salt and one tsp. vanilla. Beat until thick. Bake at 350 degrees for 45 minutes. Heat oven to 350 degrees first. Mix butter, flour, sugar and salt like pie crust. Add yolk and mix. Pat this in an 11x7 pan. Pat dough half-way up the sides. I use one can of cherries; spread cherries on the mix above. Beat your eggs till somewhat thick and add sugar gradually like a meringue. Add salt and vanilla until thick and pour over cherries.

Grandma's Best Recipes

Cherries in the Snow
Beat 6 egg whites until stiff (eggs at room temperature).
Add 2 tsp cream of tartar.
Fold in 2 cups sugar.
2 cups broken soda crackers
2/3 cups chopped nuts
Place in greased 9x13 pan

Bake 25-30 minutes at 325 degrees
Cool. Spread with Cool Whip and 1 can cherry pie filling.

Death by Chocolate
1 large chocolate cake mix
2 boxes instant chocolate pudding
1 large cool whip
Toffee Bars – 2 pkgs. (Skor)
Chill for at least 2-3 hours.

Bake cake. Cool in refrigerator. Cut up into small pieces. Make instant pudding using 3 cups only of milk (instead of the four). Start with cake and layer in glass dish with the chocolate pudding and cool whip. Sprinkle with toffee bits throughout the layers, saving some for topping. On top put cool whip then sprinkle with bites.

Cherry Dessert
8 oz. cream cheese
1 cup powdered sugar
1 pack Dream Whip
1 can cherry mix
1 graham cracker crust
Cream Cheese and powdered sugar. Whip Dream Whip and mix.

Grandma's Best Recipes

Fruit Cocktail Pie
Melt:
14 marshmallows
½ cup milk
1 cup whipping cream added when cool.
1 can fruit cocktail

Pour into graham cracker crust.

Frozen Lemon Dessert (pie)
6 oz. frozen lemonade
14 oz. can sweetened condensed milk
8 oz. Cool Whip

Combine all ingredients. Pour into a 9 inch graham cracker crust. Allow to set. May garnish with graham cracker crumbs.

Banana Cream Pie
3 tbsp. cornstarch
1 2/3 cup water
1 Eagle Brand Milk
3 egg yolks beaten
2 tbsp. oleo
Vanilla
3 bananas
Real lemon

Dissolve cornstarch in water. Stir in Eagle Brand Milk and egg yolks. Cook until bubbly and thick. Remove from heat. Add vanilla and oleo. Put sliced bananas in real lemon first then in piecrust. Put half of pudding then more bananas and rest of pudding and chill four hours. Use Dream Whip or cream on top.

Grandma's Best Recipes

Creamy Lemon Meringue Pie
3 eggs separated
1 14oz can Eagle Brand Sweetened Condensed Milk
½ cup real lemon juice (in the green bottle)
1 tsp grated lemon rind
1 graham cracker crust
¼ tsp cream of tartar
1/3 cup sugar

Preheat oven to 350 degrees. In medium bowl beat egg yolks stir in sweetened condensed milk, Real Lemon, and rind. Pour into crust. In small bowl beat egg whites with cream of tartar until foamy. Gradually add sugar beating until stiff but not dry. Spread meringue on top of pie sealing carefully to the edge of the crust. Bake 15 minutes or until meringue is golden brown. Cool. Chill before serving. Refrigerate leftovers.

Fruit Pizza
Crust:
½ cup margarine
1 cup flour
1/3 cup powdered sugar
Soften margarine; mix to form soft dough. Pat into 12 inch pizza pan. Bake 10-12 minutes at 350 degrees. Cool.

Filling:
8 oz. cream cheese (light)
½ cup powdered sugar

Soften cheese and mix all together. Spread on cooled crust. Top with fruit of your choice: bananas, grapes, strawberries, kiwi, melon, coconut, mini chocolate chips, crushed pineapple. Cut into serving pieces.

Grandma's Best Recipes

Fruit Pizza #2
1 roll sugar cookie dough
Put on a pizza pan (overlap).
Bake 12 minutes and cool.
8 oz. cream cheese
1/3 cup sugar
1 tsp vanilla
Spread on top of cookie. Add fruit.
Topping:
½ cup apricot jam. Thin with 2 tbsp. water. Drizzle on top of fruit.

Mandel Skarpar – Swedish Rusks
½ cup butter
½ cup sugar
1 beaten egg
½ tsp vanilla or almond
1 ¾ cup sifted flour
1 tsp baking powder
2 tbsp. milk

Cream sugar and butter until very light. Add beaten egg and flour which has been sifted with baking powder. Add milk and flavoring. Work well together. Spread in 2 bread loaf pans (flat loaves). Bake at 350 degrees for about 30 minutes. Cut into oblong strips while warm and place in oven with heat off to dry.

Grandma's Best Recipes

Rhubarb Dream Dessert
1 cup sifted flour
5 tbsp. confectioner's sugar
½ cup butter
Press mixture into an ungreased 7 ½ x 11 x ½ inch pan. Bake 350 degrees for 15 minutes.
Topping – Mix:
2 beaten eggs
1 ½ cups sugar
¼ cup flour
¾ tsp salt
2 cups finely chopped rhubarb

Spoon onto crust and bake 35 minutes at 350 degrees. Serve warm with whipped or plain cream. Serves 6.

Ice Cream Sandwiches
½ cup corn syrup
½ cup peanut butter
4 cups Kellog's rice krispies cereal
1 pint ice cream, cut into six slices

In medium size mixing bowl, stir together corn syrup and peanut butter. Add rice krispies cereal. Stir until well coated. Press mixture evenly in buttered 13x9x2 pan. Place in freezer or coldest part of refrigerator until firm. Cut cereal mixture into 12 3-inch squares. Sandwich each slice of ice cream between 2 squares. Freeze until firm. Cut each large sandwich in half and wrap individually in foil. Store in freezer until needed.

Grandma's Best Recipes

Date and Orange Muffins
2 cups sifted flour
3 tsps. baking powder
½ tsp salt
1 egg
¾ cup milk
¼ cup grated orange peel
¼ cup melted shortening
1 cup chopped dates

Preheat oven to 425 degrees. Grease 12x2 ½ inch muffin pan. Sift dry ingredients. Beat egg until frothy and add remaining ingredients. Make a well in flour mixture. Stir quickly – don't beat. Bake 25 minutes or until toothpicks comes out clean.

Cherry Bars
Cream together:
1 cup oleo
1 ¾ cup sugar
4 eggs
1 tsp vanilla
Add:
2 ½ cup flour
½ tsp salt
1 ½ tsp baking powder

Reserve 1 ½ cup batter. Put in jelly roll pan. Spread 1 can cherry pie filling (or another flavor of your choice) over batter. Drop reserve batter on pie filling. Smooth with knife. Bake 20-25 minutes at 350 degrees. Drizzle with powdered sugar icing.

Ice Cream Jell-O Dessert
1 package lime Jell-O
¾ cup boiling water

Drain small can pineapple juice – use juice and fill with water to make one cup. Put in 1 pint ice cream. Set 15 minutes. Add pineapple and nuts.

Pineapple Zucchini Bread – Theresa Seabloom
3 eggs
2 cups sugar
¾ cup oil
2 tsp vanilla
1 tsp salt
Beat all well and add:
2 cups shredded zucchini
1 20 oz. can crushed pineapple, drained
3 ¼ cups flour
2 tsp soda
½ tsp baking powder
1 ½ tsp cinnamon
¾ tsp nutmeg
(1 cup raisins, nuts or dates – optional)
Bake at 350 degrees over one hour. Grease and flour 2 loaf pans or three smaller ones ¾ full.

Grandma's Best Recipes

Zucchini Bread –Margaret Musson
3 eggs
1 cup oil
2 cups sugar
2 cups flour
2 cups grated zucchini
1 tsp baking soda
1 tsp salt
2 tsp vanilla
3 tsp cinnamon

Combine ingredients, grease and flour pan, bake at 350 degrees for one hour or until toothpick placed in center comes out clean

Date and Chocolate Bread
1 cup water
2 squares chocolate
Heat and stir until melted then add:
1 cup chopped dates
Simmer till soft.
Add:
1 tsp soda and cool.
Cream together:
1 cup sugar
1 egg
1 tsp vanilla
2 ¼ cups flour
¼ tsp salt
1 tsp baking powder
½ cup nuts

Bake 50-60 minutes at 350 degrees.
Makes 5 soup cans – If these are used, bake 40 minutes.

Grandma's Best Recipes

Zucchini Chocolate Cake
1 ¾ cup sugar
½ cup butter
½ cup salad oil
½ cup sour cream
2 eggs
1 tsp vanilla
2 ½ cups flour
¼ cup cocoa
1 tsp soda
1 tsp salt
½ tsp baking powder
2 cups zucchini (peeled and shredded fine)
½ cup chocolate chips
½ cup nutmeats

Cream sugar, butter, and salad oil until light. Add sour cream, eggs, vanilla. Beat well. Stir dry ingredients together into creamed mixture. Beat well. Stir in zucchini. Pour into greased and floured 9x13 pan. Bake at 325 degrees for 45 minutes, or until done.

Grandma's Best Recipes

Crème de Mente Bars
Melt and cool:
½ cup butter
4 tbsp. cocoa
Beat until smooth.
Add and Mix:
½ cup sifted powdered sugar
1 egg beaten
1 tsp vanilla
2 cups graham cracker crumbs
¾ cups chopped nuts
1 cup coconut flakes
Press this mixture into a 9x13 pan and refrigerate 1-2 hours.

Mix together and beat until smooth:
½ cup melted butter
3 tbsp. green Crème de Mente
2 tbsp. dry instant vanilla pudding
2 cups sifted powdered sugar

Spread on cooled mixture and refrigerate again for 1-2 hours. Last of all melt ¼ cup butter, 1 cup semi-sweet chocolate chips and spread on the above. Store in refrigerator or freeze. Warm at room temperature slightly to cut.

Grandma's Best Recipes

Chocolate Chip Pudding Cookies
2 ¼ cups un-sifted all-purpose flour
1 tsp soda
1 cup butter or oleo
¼ cup granulated sugar
¾ cup firmly packed brown sugar
1 package (4 oz.) Jell-O Instant pudding mix – chocolate or vanilla
1 tsp vanilla
2 eggs
1 package chocolate chips
Nuts – optional

Mix flour and soda. Combine sugars, pudding mix and vanilla. Beat till creamy. Beat in eggs, gradually add flour. Bake at 375 degrees for 8-10 minutes.

Almond Spritz – Jeano Seabloom
1 cup oleo
¾ cup sugar
1 egg
2 ¼ cup sifted flour
½ tsp baking powder
Dash of salt
1 tsp almond extract

Cream shortening. Add sugar gradually. Add egg unbeaten. Then sifted dry ingredients and almond extract.

For Bar cookies, pat into a pan ¼ inch thick. Bake and cut when cool. Can be used as cutouts. Frost lightly. (This is one of the recipes my mom used with a cookie press – Sarah)

Grandma's Best Recipes

Lemon Squares
Crust:
1 cup flour
½ cup butter
¼ cup powdered sugar
Mix like piecrust
9x9 pan 350 degrees for 15 minutes – cool
Filling:
2 beaten eggs
1 cup sugar
2 tbsp. lemon juice
Grated rind of one lemon.

Mix and pour over baked crust. Bake at 350 degrees for 20-25 minutes. Let set. Cool. Sprinkle with powdered sugar.

Delicious Cookies
1 cup white sugar
1 cup brown sugar
1 cup butter or oleo
1 cup cooking oil
1 cup rice krispies
1 cup oatmeal
1 cup coconut
1 egg
1 tsp vanilla
3 ½ cups flour
1 tsp soda
2 tsp cream of tartar
½ cup nuts

Roll into balls the size of a walnut. Flatten a little with hand. Bake at 375 degrees for 10-12 minutes.

Grandma's Best Recipes

Custard Frosting
Cook Together:
1/3 cup sugar
1/3 cup corn starch
1 egg yolk
Vanilla
Cool.

Beat together:
1 cup powdered sugar and ½ cup oleo. Mix with top mixture.

Dream Whip Frosting
1 package Dream Whip
1 cup milk
1 package instant pudding

Cherry Dessert
2 cups graham cracker crumbs
4 tbsp. sugar
½ cup butter
40 marshmallows
1 ½ cups milk
1 ½ cups whipping cream
1 can cherry pie filling

Mix first three together. Pat in ¾ of the mix into bottom of 10x10 pan. Melt marshmallows in milk. Fold cream into marshmallow mix. Pour ½ over crust. Spread with filling. Cover with rest of crumbs. Chill before serving.

Grandma's Best Recipes

Dips & Snacks

Grandma's Best Recipes

And when the woman saw that the tree was good for food, and that it was pleasant to the eyes, and a tree to be desired to make one wise, she took of the fruit thereof, and did eat, and gave also unto her husband with her; and he did eat.

Genesis 3:6   The Holy Bible. King James Version

Dips & Snacks

Vegetable Dip
1 cup Hellmann's mayonnaise
1 cup sour cream
2 tbsp. dill weed
2 tbsp. Lawry's seasoned salt
2 tbsp. parsley
2 tsp onion flakes

Mom's Christmas Meatballs
1 pound hamburger
1 package onion soup mix
2 tsp Worcestershire Sauce
1 small can evaporated milk
 Sauce:
2 cups catsup
1 cup brown sugar
1 tbsp. Worcestershire Sauce

Preheat oven to 450 degrees. Mix meat, onion soup mix, 2 tsp Worcestershire Sauce and evaporated milk. Make small meatballs with floured hands and place on cookie sheet. Bake 10 minutes. While meatballs are cooking, mix sauce ingredients in large saucepan. Add meatballs to sauce and heat until sauce is warmed. Serve in fondue or chafing dish. Makes 25 meatballs.

Grandma's Best Recipes

Cheese and Shrimp Cracker Spread
1 8 oz. package Cream Cheese
1 bottle shrimp sauce
1 can shrimp, chopped fine

Place cheese on plate. Pour sauce over top. Sprinkle with shrimp and serve with assorted crackers.

Cocktail Rye Snack
1 cup mayo
1 cup cheddar cheese
1 cup mozzarella cheese
½ cup green olives
½ cup ripe olives
Onion to taste

On small cocktail rye bread, spoon 1 tsp. on to each slice. Bake 8-10 minutes at 400 degrees.

Fish Balls
1 16 oz. can salmon, drained, boned and flaked
1 8 oz. package cream cheese
3 tsp lemon juice
1 tsp horseradish
¼ tsp liquid smoke
¼ tsp salt
3 tbsp. parsley flakes

Combine and make a ball. Roll in ½ cup pecans or whatever nuts you prefer. Chill in refrigerator overnight.

Grandma's Best Recipes

Bread and Dip
8 oz. sour cream
8 oz. mayonnaise
1 tsp dry parsley
¼ lb. Budding chopped beef
2 tsp minced onion
Dash of Worcestershire Sauce
Dash of garlic salt
Dill weed to taste
Round loaf of rye bread

Mix all ingredients together. (Make several hours ahead.) Use a round loaf of rye. Cut top off and pick pieces of bread out of center and save. Put dip in loaf and use bread pieces for dipping.

Dip
2 8-ounce cream cheese
1 1/3 cup mayonnaise
1 package Original Hidden Valley mix
Mix together and use as a spread or raw veggie dip.

Shrimp Dip
1 cream cheese – large
1 can shrimp
½ tsp mayonnaise
Milk
Drop of Worcestershire Sauce
Garlic salt

Apple Cider
Heat apple cider with cinnamon sticks and ground ginger.

Grandma's Best Recipes

Taco Dip – Sarah Rodefeld- Sarah's most requested dip
1 package 1/3 reduced fat cream cheese
Taco Seasoning – 2 tbsp. or to taste
2 tbsp. milk
Mix all together using a hand mixer and spread onto dinner plate. Set aside.

Cut up:
1 large tomato
1 small onion
2 cups finely diced lettuce (or enough to cover size of plate used for cheese mix)

Additional items needed:
1 8 oz. package finely shredded cheddar or Mexican blend cheese
1 jar of jalapeño peppers (optional)
1 bag of tortilla chips

Top the cream cheese mixture in the following order:
Lettuce, onion, tomatoes and cheese. If you use jalapeños, layer on top of the cheese. I use Tam jalapeños for less heat.

Grandma's Best Recipes

Breads, Pancakes, etc.

Grandma's Best Recipes

And take thou unto thee of all food that is eaten, and thou shalt gather it to thee; and it shall be for food for thee, and for them.

Genesis 6:21 The Holy Bible, King James Version

Grandma's Best Recipes

Breads, Pancakes, etc.

Six-Week Muffins
Put in Large bowl:
1 15 oz. box Raisin Bran
3 cups white sugar
5 cups flour
5 tsp soda
2 tsp salt
Add four eggs (beaten), 1 cup oil and 1 quart buttermilk. Mix well. Store in covered dish in refrigerator and use as desired. Do not remix. Fill cupcakes 2/3 full and bake at 400 degrees for 15-20 minutes. Keeps six weeks. More raisins can be added.

Lefse
Boil potatoes with jackets. Peel while hot and rice – cool. Best to use Russets or Burbanks.
8 cups riced potatoes
2 cups flour
¼ cup salad oil
1 tbsp. salt
Little sugar

Stir four into potato mixture. Pull off pieces of the dough and turn into walnut size balls. Lightly flour a pastry cloth, and roll out lefse balls to 1/8 in thickness. Cook on a hot (400 degree F/200 C) griddle until bubbles form and each side has browned. Place on damp towel to cool sightly, and then cover with damp towel until ready to serve.

Use ¼ cup dough to roll at one time.

Grandma's Best Recipes

Roll Dough
1 cup scalded milk
½ cup Crisco
½ cup sugar
3 eggs
1 level tsp salt
2 pkgs. dry yeast
4 ½ cups flour
Rest 15 minutes
Bake 20 minutes at 375 degrees.

One Egg Cake for Shortcake
½ cup sugar
1 egg – beaten
3 tbsp. shortening
½ cup sweet milk
1 ½ cup sifted flour
2 ½ tsp baking powder
Few grains of salt
1 tsp vanilla
½ tsp lemon extract

To creamed shortening, add sugar and egg alternately. Add milk and sifted flour with salt and baking powder. Add extract. Bake in greased and floured 8x8x2 pan in a moderate oven for 30 minutes.

Grandma's Best Recipes

Poppy Seed Bread
1 large yellow cake mix
4 eggs
½ cup oil
¾ cup hot water
2 tsps. grated orange rind
½ cup sifted flour
½ cup orange juice
¼ cup poppy seeds
1 cup chopped walnuts

Put all ingredients in bowl. Beat 4 minutes. Pour into greased and floured loaf pans. Bake at 350 degrees for 50 minutes. Can be frozen.

Grandma's Best Recipes

Bread Pudding
6 cups milk
Day old bread cut into 2 inch cubes – about 12 cups
¾ cup melted butter
1 ½ cups sugar
6 eggs, slightly beaten
¾ tsp salt
1 ½ cups raisin
3 tsp cinnamon
Dash of nutmeg
Hard Sauce for Bread Pudding:
2 cups sugar
1 cup butter
½ cup water
2 eggs beaten
6 tbsp. lemon juice

Scald milk then pour over bread. Let set until cool. Preheat oven to 375 degrees. Add butter, sugar, eggs, salt, raisins cinnamon and nutmeg to milk and bread mixture. Pour mixture into greased 9x13 pan. Bake 1 hour and 15 minutes or until knife inserted in center comes out clean. Serve with hard sauce.

Grandma's Best Recipes

Monkey Bread
3 tubes biscuits
½ tsp cinnamon
½ cup sugar
Nuts
1 ½ sticks oleo
1tsp. cinnamon
1 cup brown sugar

Cut biscuits into 4 pieces. Roll each piece in mixture of ½ tsp. cinnamon and 1/3 cup sugar. Grease Bundt pan. Place nuts in bottom of pan then layer the biscuits. Combine oleo, 1 tsp. cinnamon and brown sugar. Boil 2-3 minutes. Pour over biscuits and nuts. Bake 350 for 25 minutes.

Swedish Pancakes
1 cup flour
2 tbsp. sugar
¼ tsp salt
3 eggs
3 cups milk

Sift flour into bowl; Add sugar and salt. Then add eggs and milk gradually, stirring until well blended, and let stand two hours. Heat Swedish pancake pan (or ordinary pancake pan) and butter well. Beat batter again, pour by tablespoonfuls into sections of pan and fry on both sides until nicely brown. Place on very hot platter and serve immediately with Ligonberries.

Grandma's Best Recipes

Blueberry Pancakes
1 package blueberry muffin mix
1 cup flour
1 tsp baking powder
1 cup water
1 egg
1 tbsp. oil

Empty blueberries into strainer. Wash under cold water. Set aside to drain. In medium bowl, blend muffin mix, flour and baking powder with a fork. Stir in slightly beaten egg, water and oil. Mix until blended. Stir in blueberries. Makes 12-4½ inch pancakes.

Zucchini Pancakes
2 cups zucchini
¼ cup shredded cheese
½ cup Bisquick
2 eggs
Salt and pepper

Sour Cream Pancakes
2 cups Bisquick
1 egg
¾ cup cold water
2/3 cup sour cream

Beat all ingredients together until smooth. Make about 18 4-inch pancakes.

Grandma's Best Recipes

Thin Pancakes – Grandpa's favorite.
½ cup flour
¾ cup milk
2 tbsp. melted butter
4 egg yolks
½ tsp salt
2 tsp sugar
1 tsp baking powder
4 egg whites

Beat flour and milk together for 12-15 minutes (yes, minutes…) Add melted butter. Beat egg yolks for ten minutes (yes minutes) and add to flour and milk mixture. Add salt, sugar, and baking powder and the stiffly beaten egg whites. Fry in medium size skillet. You may roll with jelly and cover with powdered sugar.

Otto's Pancakes
6 eggs
1 cup milk
4 tsp sugar
Salt
6 heaping tsp flour
Best to stand overnight

Pancakes
1 cup buttermilk
2 slices crumbled bread
2 eggs
Salt
2 tsp melted butter
½ tsp baking soda
1 tsp baking powder
Flour for right consistency

Grandma's Best Recipes

Fluffy Pancakes
1 cup all-purpose flour
1 tbsp. sugar
2 tsp. baking powder
½ tsp salt
¾ cup milk
1 egg
¼ cup shortening, melted
In a bowl, combine flour, sugar, baking powder and salt. Combine milk, egg and shortening. Stir into dry ingredients and mix well. Pour batter by ¼ cupful on to a lightly greased hot griddle. Turn when bubbles form on top of pancakes. Cook until second side is golden brown. Makes eight pancakes.

Fluffy Cakes
1 egg
¾ cup plus 2 tbsp. milk
2 tbsp. melted shortening or salad oil
1 cup enriched flour
½ tsp salt
2 tbsp. baking powder
2 tbsp. sugar

Combine egg, milk and shortening. Add sifted dry ingredients and beat until smooth. Bake on ungreased griddle. Pour batter from ¼ cup measurer. Makes 12 small cakes. For smooth golden brown cakes, season the griddle with salt. You won't need to grease it. Put 1-2 tbsp. salt in a small cheesecloth bag. Rub over griddle. Repeat salt treatment after every batch during baking.

Grandma's Best Recipes

Alminnelige Vafler (Norwegian Sweet Waffles)
4 eggs, beaten
2 cups sugar
4 cups sweet milk
1 tsp soda dissolved in a little sour milk or cream
4 cups sifted flour
1 tbsp. melted butter (if cream is noted used)

Mix in order named. Makes 20-24 waffles. May be eaten warm but are especially good cold and served with butter or jam or jelly.

Never Fail Rolls
1 cup scaled milk
1 ½ pkgs. dry yeast
½ cup sugar
3 well-beaten eggs
½ cp vegetable shortening
½ cup lukewarm water
1 tsp salt
5 cups enriched flour

Mix, cover and let rise in greased bowl until doubled in size (or more). Divide dough into three equal parts and roll into pie shapes ½ inch thick on floured board. Cut each pie shape into quarters and each quarter into thirds. Begin at large end and roll into rolls. Place on greased cookie sheet and let rise until size doubles. Bake about 13 minutes in 375-degree oven until golden brown. Brush tops with butter.

Grandma's Best Recipes

Swedish Limpa Bread
2 packages active dry yeast
1 ½ cups warm water – 105 to 115 degrees
¼ cup molasses
1/3 cup sugar
1 tbsp. salt
2 tbsp. shortening
Grated peel of 1 to 2 oranges or tsp of anise seed
2 ½ cups medium rye flour
2 ¼ to 2 ¾ cups gold medal flour cornmeal

In mixing bowl, dissolve yeast in warm water. Stir in molasses, sugar, salt, shortening, orange peel and rye flour. Beat until smooth. Mix in enough white flour to make dough easy to handle.
Turn dough onto lightly floured board. Cover and let rest 10 – 15 minutes – this makes dough easier to handle. Knead until smooth, about five minutes. Place in greased bowl. Turn greased side up. Cover, let rise in warm place until double, about one hour. Punch down dough, round up, cover and let rise until double, about 40 minutes. Grease baking sheet and sprinkle with cornmeal. Punch down dough. Divide in half. Shape each half into round loaves. Cover and let rise one hour. Heat oven to 375 degrees and bake 30 - 35 minutes.

Grandma's Best Recipes

Fix and Mix Bread
3 ¾ cup warm water
3 packages dry yeast
6 tablespoons sugar
6 tablespoons melted oleo
4 tsp salt
10 cups flour

Add yeast to warm water and stir until dissolved. Add the sugar, oleo, salt and flour. Mix all real good. Put seal on bowl real tight and burp to let air out. Put in warm place and wait 30 minutes. Divide dough and put in greased pans. Cover with towel and wait 30 minutes. Bake at 350 degrees for 30 minutes.

Poppy Seed Bread
4 eggs
2 cups sugar
1 ½ cup oil
1 tsp salt
1 can evaporated milk
3 cups flour
1 ½ tsp baking powder
1 tsp vanilla
1 tsp almond & 1 can Solo almond or poppy seed filling
Nuts (optional)

Bake at 350 degrees, 1 hour

Glaze:
¼ cup orange juice
¾ cup sugar
½ tsp vanilla
½ tsp almond
1 tsp butter

Grandma's Best Recipes

Mexican Corn Bread
1 cup yellow cornmeal
½ cup all-purpose flour
2 tbsp. sugar
1 tsp salt
2 tsp baking powder
½ tsp baking soda
2 eggs beaten
1 cup buttermilk
½ cup vegetable oil
1 can (8 ¾ oz.) cream style corn
1/3 cup chopped onion
2 tbsp. chopped green pepper
½ cup shredded cheddar cheese

In a mixing bowl, combine first six ingredients. Combine remaining ingredients; add to dry ingredients and stir only until moistened. Pour into a greased 9-inch square baking pan or 10 inch heavy skillet. Bake at 350 degrees for 30-35 minutes, or until bread is golden brown and tests done.

Swedish Soft Flat Bread
½ cup shortening
½ cup sugar
2 eggs
½ cup buttermilk
½ cup sweet milk
1 tsp baking soda
1 tsp baking powder
5 – 5 ½ cups flour

Cut and bake in electric fry pan.

Grandma's Best Recipes

Breadsticks
Cut dough into 24 pieces. On a lightly floured board roll each piece in between your palms into a rope that is 8 inches long. Place 2-3 inches apart in greased baking sheets. Cover and let rise in a warm place until nearly double (about 30 minutes). Beat together 1 egg white and 1 tbsp. water and brush over bread sticks. Sprinkle with sesame seeds. Bake at 375 degrees for 10 minutes. Reduce temperature to 300 and bake for 20-25 minutes more. Cool.

Coffee Cake
4 cups flour
1 cup butter or oleo
1 yeast cake
Mix like piecrust.
Add:
2 eggs
4 tbsp. sugar
1 cup warm water, beat and let stand in refrigerator overnight.
Filling:
2 cups brown sugar
1 cup graham crackers
¾ cups nuts

Roll dough and cover with filling. Roll up and seal ends. Makes 2. Bake 350 for 25 minutes. Ice with thin cover of powdered sugar icing.

Grandma's Best Recipes

Rhubarb Bread
3 eggs
1 cup oil
2 cups brown sugar
2 ½ cups rhubarb finely chopped
½ cup chopped nuts, optional
½ tsp grated orange zest
3 cups flour
2 tsp baking soda
½ tsp baking powder
2 tsp cinnamon
1 tsp salt
Dash of nutmeg
Cinnamon and sugar mixture, optional

Preheat oven to 350 degrees. Grease two 5x9 bread pans. Beat eggs oil, brown sugar and vanilla (vanilla was not listed in the ingredients) until thick and foamy. Stir in rhubarb, nuts and orange zest. Set aside. In another bowl, sift flour, baking soda, baking powder, cinnamon, salt and nutmeg. Stir into reserved egg mixture. Pour into prepared pans. Sprinkle with a mixture of cinnamon and sugar, if desired. Bake one hour and cool on rack for ten minutes before removing from pan.

Grandma's Best Recipes

Date and Nut Bread
Cup of one package of dates
½ tsp soda
1 ½ cup boiling water
--
1 cup sugar
½ cup shortening
2 eggs
Cream above three ingredients
--
Add date liquid
2 ¾ cup flour
2 tsp baking powder
Salt
1 tsp vanilla
Add dates and nuts

Bake 350 degrees for 45 minutes
Makes two loaves.

Popcorn Cake
Melt together:
½ cup margarine
½ cup shortening
1 10-ounce bag miniature marshmallows
Mix together:
4 quarts popcorn
½ - ¾ cup of nuts, gumdrops and M&Ms

Pour the melted mixture over the popcorn mixture. Press into a tube or Bundt pan. Allow time to set.

Grandma's Best Recipes

Cherry Cake
1 package cake mix
3 eggs
1 can pie filling
Use strawberry for white cake – use chocolate cake and cherry filling.

Bake according to cake directions

Original Toll House Cookies
Preheat oven to 375 degrees
Sift together:
2 ¼ cups flour
1 tsp baking soda
1 tsp salt
Set aside.
Combine:
1 cup softened butter or shortening
¾ cup white sugar
¾ cup brown sugar
1 tsp vanilla
½ tsp water
Beat until creamy.

Beat in two eggs. Add flour mixture and mix well. Stir in one 12 oz. package of chocolate chips, 1 cup chopped nuts. Drop by spoonfuls on greased cookie sheet. Bake 375 degrees for 10-12 minutes. Nuts can be omitted. Variations – add four cups crisp ready to eat cereal or add 2 cups chopped dates.

Grandma's Best Recipes

Chocolate Star Cookies
1 ¾ cups flour
1 tsp baking soda
½ tsp salt
½ cup butter
½ cup peanut butter
½ cup white sugar
½ cup brown sugar
1 egg
1 tsp vanilla

Form into balls and roll in white sugar. Bake 375 degrees for 8 minutes. Put chocolate stars in center of each and press down. Bake another 2-3 minutes.

Apple Pudding
Peel, pare and place quartered apples in deep dish baking pan.
Sauce:
1 cup sugar
2 tbsp. flour
2 tbsp. butter
½ cup water
Cook until clear. Add vanilla.

Pour over apples in baking dish and bake 25 minutes in a 375-degree oven.

Grandma's Best Recipes

Apple Squares
2 eggs beaten
1 cup sugar
1 cup brown sugar
1 cup flour
2 tsp baking powder
1 tsp vanilla
2 cups apples (chopped)
1 cup nuts (chopped)

Bake 40 minutes at 350 degrees in a 9 x 12 pan.

Cherry Marlo
2 cups crushed graham crackers
4 tbsp. sugar
½ cup oleo
Mix together and put ¾ of mixture into bottom of 9x13 pan.
40 marshmallows
1 ½ cup milk
1 large cool whip
1 can cherry pie filling

Melt marshmallows in milk over low heat and cool. Fold cool whip into marshmallow mixture. Pour ½ mixture over crust. Put cherry pie filling over mixture. Cover with other half of marshmallow mix. Refrigerate. Just before serving, sprinkle on rest of cracker crumbs.

Grandma's Best Recipes

Sour Cream Nut Bread
2 cups sifted flour
1 tsp baking powder
1 tsp soda
1 tsp salt
¼ tsp cinnamon
¼ tsp cloves (optional)
¼ tsp nutmeg
1 egg beaten
1 cup brown sugar
1 cup sour cream
1 cup nut meats
2 tbsp. butter

Sift dry ingredients together. Beat eggs slightly. Add sugar and beat until thick. Stir in sour cream and butter. Add dry ingredients stirring only to moisten. Add nuts. Pour in loaf pan and bake 350 degrees for one hour.

Orange Bread
3 cups flour
4 tsp baking powder
½ tsp salt
½ cup sugar
Chopped nuts
½ cup candied orange peel
1 cup milk
1 egg

Sift dry ingredients. Add nuts and chopped orange peel. Add milk with well-beaten eggs. Put in greased bread pan. Stand 10 minutes. Bake in moderate oven at 350 degrees for 34 minutes.

Grandma's Best Recipes

Maraschino Cherry Nut Bread
1 ½ cup sugar
½ cup shortening
¼ cup cherry juice from maraschino cherries
2 ½ cups flour
½ cup milk
1 cup nuts chopped
3 eggs
½ cup maraschino cherries cut fine or 10 oz. jar
2 tbsp. baking powder, 1 tsp vanilla
1 tsp vanilla

Cream together sugar and shortening. Add eggs. Combine juices and milk. Add flour mixture and liquid alternately to first mixture. Fold in cherries, nuts and vanilla. Bake 1 hour at 350 degrees. Grease and flour pans. Makes 2 small loaves 8 ½ x 4 ½ x 2 5/8 inch.

Pumpkin Crèmes – Sarah's most requested fall cookie.
1 cup sugar
½ cup butter
1 egg
1 tsp soda, 1 tsp baking powder
1 tsp cinnamon
1 tsp salt
1 cup canned pumpkin
2 cups flour

Mix sugar and margarine. Add egg and mix just until mixed. Add soda, cinnamon, salt and powder. Add pumpkin and mix just until blended. Add flour and mix well making sure to scrape the bottom of the bowl to ensure everything is mixed well. Drop by rounded teaspoon onto baking sheet (I use stoneware which does not need to be greased). Bake 10-15 minutes at 350 degrees. Remove onto racks to cool. Frost with powdered sugar frosting. The cookies freeze well – frost after thawing.

Grandma's Best Recipes

Side Dishes

Grandma's Best Recipes

And let them gather all the food of those good years that come, and lay up corn under the hand of Pharaoh, and let them keep food in the cities.

Genesis 41:35 The Holy Bible, King James Version

Grandma's Best Recipes

Side Dishes

Potatoes Deluxe (Margaret Anderson Musson)
2 Pounds Hash browns (thaw 30 minutes)
1 cup onions - diced
1 cup cream of chicken
1 pound sour cream
½ cup oleo – melted
8 oz. sharp cheese (grated)
Salt and pepper
Mix all together

Bake 375 one hour (12-15 people)

Escalloped Asparagus
2 cans asparagus (drained cuts and tips)
1 can mushroom soup
¼ pound cheese

Place drained asparagus in flat baking dish. Use liquid and water to dilute soup. Heat and melt cheese in soup. Pour over asparagus. Top with buttered crumbs. Bake 30 minutes in moderate oven.

Grandma's Best Recipes

Veggies and Onion Casserole
1 sliced onion
2 medium new potatoes, sliced
2 medium yellow crook neck squash, sliced
1 stick butter
Salt and pepper to taste

Melt butter. In a 2 ½ quart casserole dish, layer potatoes, carrots, onion and squash. Top with a layer of green tomatoes. After each layer add salt and pepper and some butter. Bake in oven at 325 degrees for one hour.

Rice with Black Beans
1 medium onion chopped
1 tbsp. oil
1 14 ½ ounce can of stewed tomatoes
1 16 oz. can black beans, undrained
½ tsp dried oregano leaves
½ tsp garlic powder
1 ½ cups Minute Instant Brown Rice

Cook and stir onion in hot oil in saucepan until tender but not browned. Add tomatoes beans, oregano and garlic powder. Bring to boil. Stir in rice. Return to boil. Reduce heat; cover and simmer five minutes. Remove from heat and let stand five minutes. Makes 8 servings.

Grandma's Best Recipes

Rhubarb Salad
3 cups cut up Rhubarb
2 cups diced celery
2 cups cold water
2 packages small strawberry Jell-O
½ cup sugar
¼ tsp salt
¼ cup lemon juice

Cook rhubarb, sugar and salt in pan until tender (don't stir or add water). Add other ingredients and chill. You may add chopped nuts to this.

Vegetable Relish
1 can green beans (French or cuts)
1 can tiny sweet peas
1 can white corn (I used yellow)
½ cup chopped onion
½ cup chopped celery
½ cup chopped green or red pepper
½ cup vinegar
½ cup sugar
1/3 cup oil
Salt and pepper to taste

Mix vegetables in large bowl. Make dressing for remaining ingredients and pour over. Let marinate over nigh in refrigerator.

Grandma's Best Recipes

Broccoli Casserole
Sauté:
2/3 cups chopped onion
½ cup chopped celery
1 box frozen broccoli
Add 1 can cream of mushroom soup
1 can cream of chicken soup

Mix well. Stir in 1 cup grated cheddar cheese. Bring to a boil. Add 1 ½ cup minute rice, uncooked. Put in a buttered casserole dish. Put buttered bread crumbs on top. Bake 1 hour at 350 degrees (covered).

Copper Pennies
5 cups sliced carrots
1 medium onion
1 green pepper
1 can tomato soup
½ cup salad oil
1 cup sugar
¾ cup vinegar
1 tsp prepared mustard
1 tsp Worcestershire sauce
1 tsp salt

Cook carrots - cool. Slice onion and pepper and mix with carrots. Mix other ingredients – pour over carrots. Marinate overnight or longer. Drain and serve. Keep in refrigerator.

Grandma's Best Recipes

Spinach Bars (Nettie Anderson Musson)
1 pound Monterey Jack Cheese
1 box 10 oz. frozen spinach
3 eggs
1 cup flour
1 cup milk
Melt ½ stick oleo in 9x13 pan. Beat eggs. Add flour, milk, salt, 1 tbsp. baking powder and mix well. Add one pound cheese, one package thawed, not cooked spinach. Mix well and pour in pan. Bake 350 degrees for 35 minutes. Cut when cool.

Green Bean Dish
Brown one pound hamburger with a little onion. Put in bottom of casserole dish. Then put one can French style green beans, drained. Save ½ cup of the juice. Then add one can cream of mushroom soup, undiluted. Add juice from green beans. One cup mushrooms, one cup onion rings. Put tater tots on top. Bake 375 degrees for one hour, covered.

German Potato Salad
Boil 8 medium potatoes with jackets. Cool and peel. (Boil in four cups water, one sliced onion and ½ cup vinegar). Thicken with flour and water like gravy. Add ¾ cup sugar and salt and pepper to taste. Slice potatoes and put on mixture. Dice and fry ¾ pound of bacon and add fat and bacon to mixture.

German Potato Salad (Selma Anderson)
Boiled potatoes diced
Fry bacon, pour over potatoes
Raw onion to taste.
Dressing: two heaping spoons of Miracle Whip, one raw egg, 2 tsp vinegar. Blend and pour over potatoes.

Grandma's Best Recipes

Rice Pudding
½ cup uncooked rice
1 quart milk
¼ tsp. salt
Sugar – scant ½ cup
2 eggs
Vanilla
Cook 1 quart milk. ½ cup rice, salt and sugar. 15 minutes over low heat. Butter (tbsp.) a casserole dish. Pour in contents. Add vanilla and two beaten eggs. Bake 30 minutes at 350 degrees.

Cranberry Orange Relish
4 cups (1 pound) Ocean Spray Fresh Cranberries
2 oranges quartered and seeds removed
2 cups sugar

Put cranberries and oranges, including the rind, through the food grinder (coarse blade). Stir in the sugar and chill. Makes two pints. Keeps well for weeks stored in the refrigerator.

Grandma's Best Recipes

Country Style Cold Slaw
1 cup Hellmann's mayonnaise
3 tbsp. sugar
3 tbsp. cider vinegar
1 ½ tsp salt
¾ tsp dry mustard
¼ tsp celery seed
8 cups shredded cabbage
1 ½ cups shredded carrots
1 cup diced green pepper
¼ cup sliced green onion

In large bowl, stir together first six ingredients. Add next four ingredients, toss to coat well. Cover and chill several hours. If desired, serve in bowl lined with lettuce leaves. Makes about eight cups.

Lobster Salad
1 cup sea shell macaroni
½ cup mayonnaise,
½ cup sour cream
1 tbsp. diced pimiento
½ cup milk
½ tsp celery seed,
2 tsp minced green pepper
1 tbsp. sweet pickle relish
¼ cup finely cut celery,
 2 green onions chopped with tops
8 oz. cooked lobster (cut in cubes)
¾ cups cubed mild cheddar cheese (small cubes)

Mix all together and serve

Grandma's Best Recipes

Kraut Salad
1 15 oz. can kraut
1 green pepper chopped
2 cup celery
1 cup chopped onion
¾ cup sugar

Combine all ingredients and chill for several hours.

Lettuce Salad (layered)
1 head lettuce chopped into small pieces
1 green pepper diced
1 medium onion diced
Raw peas (tiny frozen)
Celery
8 oz. cheddar cheese
1 cup mayonnaise
1 cup cream

Layer - lettuce, peppers, onions, celery, and peas. Mix mayonnaise and sour cream. Spread like frosting. 2 tbsp. sugar on top. 8 oz. shredded cheese on top. Crumble bacon on top. Let stand overnight.

Lime Jell-O Salad
1 pkg. lime Jell-O dissolved in half cup boiling water. Add one number 2 can crushed pineapple, juice and all. One cup chopped nuts. One cup sour cream. Mix all good and set in refrigerator till set. Stir once in a while.

Grandma's Best Recipes

Russian Dill Pickles
Brine for 2 quarts.
1 ½ cup sugar
1 ½ cup white vinegar
1 ½ cup water
¼ cup canning salt
1 tbsp. pickling spice in a bag
Dill
Cucumbers

Boil brine – simmer 10 minutes and discard spices. Put cucumbers and dill in jars. Cover with brine – put in canner and bring to boil and turn off heat. Take out when cooled down. It make four qts. And the double recipe of brine and it comes out perfect. You can cut pickles length wise if they are too big.

Beet Pickles
Strain juice and save.
3 cups beet juice
2 cups vinegar
1 cup sugar

Let come to a boil. Drop pieces of beets in. Heat through. Put in jars and seal.

Cucumber in Sour Cream
2 medium peeled cucumbers
1 medium onion thinly sliced
1 ¼ tsp salt
1 cup sour cream
2 tbsp. vinegar
¼ tsp sugar
1/8 tsp paprika
1 tsp parsley flakes

Grandma's Best Recipes

Tapioca Salad
1 box minute tapioca (I use ½ box)
1 small pkg. instant vanilla pudding
1 small package orange Jell-O
2 cans mandarin oranges – drained
1 can pineapple chunks – drained
1 9 oz. Cool Whip
12 maraschino cherries – chopped

In large bowl, pour tapioca, pudding mix and gelatin. Boil three cups water and pour over mixture. Stir – Let stand 3-5 minutes. Add fruits and cool whip. Mix well. Pour into 9x12 glass dish or fancy ring mold. Put in refrigerator until firm. I also made it with two bananas, some strawberries (no sugar) and strawberry Jell-O. It's great for holidays. Could be dessert with cool whip and nuts on top.

Taco Salad
1 pound ground beef
1 package taco seasoning
Brown meat, drain fat, and mix with taco seasoning
1 medium head lettuce
1 oz. grated cheddar cheese
1 green pepper diced
1 onion diced
1 pkg. taco chips – crushed
1 tomato – diced
1 medium bottle Catalina dressing (Kraft)
Toss all together and serve

Grandma's Best Recipes

Vegetable Salad
Cauliflower
Tomatoes
Green Pepper
Celery
Onion
Radish
Garlic and Onion Salt
Equal parts vinegar, sugar, and oil.

Sauerkraut and Bacon
Brown and drain one pound of bacon with one medium chopped onion. In a bowl put:
2 pounds sauerkraut
1 cup sugar
1 cup water
2 ½ tbsp. cornstarch
2 tbsp. vinegar

Add bacon and one small package of fresh mushrooms. Mix together and bake in low cake pan at 350 degrees for 1 ½ hours.

Broccoli Salad
2 cups chopped salad
2 bunches of broccoli (floret's only)
½ cup chopped green onions or ¼ regular onion
1 pound bacon fried crisp and broken into small pieces
2 cups red or green grapes cut into ½ or 1/4s.
1 cup sliced almonds

Dressing:
2 cups salad dressing
1 scant cup sugar
2 tbsp. vinegar
Mix well and add to above ingredients.

Grandma's Best Recipes

Sliced Cucumbers
Slice cucumbers thin. Slice onions thin. Make dressing of mayonnaise, vinegar, sugar, salt and oil.

Basting Sauce for Pork
3 tbsp. lime or lemon juice
3 tbsp. salad oil
1 small garlic clove

Mixed Pickles
4 quarts cucumbers
1 quart onions
3 cups cauliflower
1 green pepper
3 cloves garlic
½ cup canning salt
Ice cubes
5 cups sugar
2 tbsp. mustard seed
½ tbsp. celery seed
1 quart cidar vinegar

Slice onions, pepper and cucumbers thin. Break up cauliflower. Combine vegetables with garlic and add salt. Cover with ice cubes. Mix and let stand 3 hours. Drain well. Combine remaining ingredients and pour over vegetables. Bring to a boil. Put in clean, hot pint jars allowing ½ inch head room. Seal and process in boiling water bath for 15 minutes. Remove jars and complete seals if necessary. Makes 8 pints.

Crab Apple Pickles (Margaret Anderson Musson)
Syrup:
1 quart vinegar
3 cups water
4 cups sugar
1 tbsp. cloves
1 tbsp. mace
1 tbsp. allspice
1 cinnamon stick

Bring to a rolling boil for one minute. Cool. Add washed apples. Heat slow not to burst apples. Stand overnight. Remove spice bag. Put in jars and add syrup. Put in water bath 20 minutes. Makes five pints.

Bleu Cheese Dressing
1-2 cups Hellmann's Mayonnaise
About ½ package of crumbled blue cheese
Add small amount of concentrated lemon juice and Worcestershire Sauce (each approximately 2 tbsp.). Mix well and let stand overnight.

Grandma's Best Recipes

Rice Vera Cruz - Prue Bloom Johnson – Jeano's sister
½ pound lean ground beef
2 medium onions, chopped
16 oz. can diced or petite diced tomatoes
1 can beef consume
½ cup dry wine
2 tsp chili powder
Salt to taste
1 cup uncooked long grain white rice or brown rice
2 cups grated cheese

Sauté beef and onion. Add tomatoes, consume, wine, chili powder and salt. Bring to boil and slowly add rice. Cover and bake at 375 degrees for 30 minutes, or 45 minutes if using brown rice. Uncover, stir, and top with cheese. Bake uncovered for an additional 15 minutes. Let stand 5-10 minutes before serving.

Kraut
1 can kraut
1 large onion
¼ to ½ cup sugar (for Reuben sandwiches)
Caraway seed and water

Put bacon fat in pan with onion. Cook until soft – drain kraut – pour water over it till water looks clean. Add to onion. Add caraway, sugar and a little water. Cook 1 ½ hours (no oven temp listed

Grandma's Best Recipes

Cold Cauliflower Salad
1 head cauliflower – washed and cut into pieces
½ cup chopped onion
½ cup thinly sliced radishes
1 cup mayonnaise
1 cup sour cream
1 pkg. (dry) good season cheese and garlic salad dressing mix

Mix all very well and put in large covered bowl. Refrigerate overnight

Lime Cream Jell-O Mold
1 package lime Jell-O
1 medium can crushed pineapple – no water

Heat Jell-O to boil with crushed pineapple. Cool pineapple and Jell-O mixture. Then add a small package of softened and creamed cream cheese and ½ pint cream whipped, beaten and thick. Fold in ½ cup nuts.

Cranberry Fruit Salad
1 pound uncooked cranberries
1 ½ cup sugar
1 Number two can pineapple tidbits
½ cup walnuts
2 cups small marshmallows
4 bananas cut up
2 cups green grapes
½ pint cream (whipped)

Grind or blend cranberries. Add sugar and let stand 2 hours. Add fruit, marshmallows and nuts. Fold in whipped cream.

Grandma's Best Recipes

Mandarin Jell-O Salad
2 pkgs. orange Jell-O
Mandarin oranges and juice (no quantity listed)
2 cups boiling water
1 cup cold water

Make Jell-O with boiling water. Add cold water, oranges and juice. Set to congeal. Add small or medium Cool Whip. Beat all together.

Chili Chicken Salad
1 ½ cup cut-up cooked chicken or turkey
1 15 ½ oz. can kidney beans – drained
2 green onions – sliced
1 small head iceberg lettuce or 10 oz. spinach, torn into bite size pieces
Mexacali dressing (recipe below):
1 medium avocado
1 cup broken tortilla chips
1 medium tomato, cut into wedges. Ripe olives

Place chicken, beans, onions and lettuce in large bowl. Cover and refrigerate at least three hours. Prepare Mexacali Dressing.

Mexacali Dressing:
½ cup mayo or salad dressing
¼ cup catsup
1 tsp chili powder
½ tsp garlic salt

Just before serving, cut avocado into bite sized pieces. Add avocado and dressing to chicken mixture. Toss. Sprinkle with tortilla chips. Garnish with tomatoes and olives.
Cheesy chicken salad – substitute ¾ cup shredded cheddar cheese or jalapeno pepper cheese (about 3 oz.) for ½ cup of the chicken.

Grandma's Best Recipes

Cabbage Slaw
½ head cabbage
1 green pepper
Onions, celery, and carrots
Equal portions vinegar and sugar. Salt to taste.

Marinated Tomatoes
3 large tomatoes
1/3 cup olive oil
¼ cup red wine vinegar
1 tsp salt
¼ tsp pepper
½ clove garlic
2 tbsp. chopped onion
1 tbsp. fresh parsley
1 tsp basil

Cheese Custard Pie
¾ pound chopped ham
3 tbsp. each diced green pepper and onion
3 tbsp. butter
2 cups grated cheese (1 cup cheddar, one cup Swiss)
2 cups milk
3 eggs beaten until blended
½ tsp salt
¼ tsp Worcestershire Sauce

Sauté ham, pepper and onion in the 3 tbsp. butter. Cool. Add to beaten eggs, milk and cheese. Mix well. Pour into a 9-inch unbaked pie shell. Bake in very hot oven (450 degrees) about 12 minutes. Reduce heat to slow oven (325 degrees) and continue to bake 35 minutes or until knife inserted in center comes out clean. Serve hot. Serves 6-8

Grandma's Best Recipes

Broccoli Casserole
2/3 cup chopped onion
½ cup chopped celery
One box frozen broccoli
Sauté above items. Add:
1 can cream of mushroom soup
1 can cream of chicken soup
Mix well and stir in:
1 cup grated cheddar cheese.

Bring to a boil and add 1 cup uncooked minute rice. Put in a buttered casserole dish. Put buttered breadcrumbs on top. Bake 1 hour at 350 degrees.

Potato Salad
Boiled potatoes – diced into small chunks
Fry bacon
Pour over potatoes
Raw onions to taste
Dressing:
2 heaping spoons miracle whip
1 raw egg
2 tsp vinegar
2 tsp sugar
Blend and pour over potatoes.

Macaroni Salad
½ pound pkg. macaroni
1 cup chopped celery
1 tsp pimento or stuffed olives
1 cup dried meat or fish
Salad dressing to moisten. Grate raw carrots or a can of peas.

Grandma's Best Recipes

Cheesy Hash Browns
2 pound package hash browns
1 large sour cream
2 tbsp. dry onions
1 stick oleo
1 cup cream of celery soup (or other cream soups)
2 cups shredded cheddar cheese
2 cups corn flakes
1 stick oleo

Put hash browns in baking dish. Heat together cheese, oleo, soup. Add onion. Pour over potatoes. Bake. Melt oleo and mix in corn flakes. Put on top ½ hour before done. Good with ham. Bake 350 degrees for one hour.

Easy Potato Pancakes
3 large eggs
¼ cup milk
1/3 cup sifted flour
1 tsp salt
½ cup fresh frozen chopped onion
2 patties frozen Ore-Ida shredded Hash Browns defrosted and separated
Butter or oleo for frying

Beat eggs, milk, flour and salt. Stir in hash browns and onions. Heat 2 tbsp. butter or oleo in skillet over medium heat. Pour in a generous ¼ cup batter for each pancake. Spread thinly to about 3 inches in diameter. Fry until golden brown and crisp. Brown other side. 10 – 3 ½ inch pancakes.

Grandma's Best Recipes

Potato Pancakes
6 grated potatoes
2/3 cup pancake mix
3 eggs
1 tsp sugar

Crepes
3 eggs, slightly beaten
6 tbsp. flour
1/3 cup milk
Butter or oleo

Beat eggs, flour and salt until smooth. Add milk and beat until smooth. Cover and chill ½ to one hour if possible. Stir batter before using. For each crepe heat about ½ tsp butter in 7-8 inch crepe pan over medium-high heat. Pour in scant ¼ cup batter quickly tilting pan to distribute batter evenly. When light on bottom, turn and lightly brown other side. Makes 12 crepes.

Cucumber Salad
8 cucumbers – peeled and cubed in ½ inch squares or slices
1 green pepper chopped
1 cup green onion chopped
1 ½ tbsp. salt
Let stand ½ hour drain well.
Mix 2 cups sugar
1 cup vinegar
1 tsp mustard seed

Let stand 20 minutes then mix all together. Let stand 24 hours. Will keep well.

Grandma's Best Recipes

Baked Beans
2 pounds navy beans
½ pound salt pork (plus ½ more)
Onion
½ cup brown sugar (plus ½ cup more)
Mustard
1 jar molasses
Bake 1 hour at 400 degrees

Reduce heat to 300 degrees
(the items above in () were added to the main recipe. No time was given for baking at 300 degrees.)

Baked Onions
4 pounds sweet onions
2 tablespoons butter
2 cups (8 oz.) shredded Swiss cheese
1 can cream of chicken soup
Mix in ½ cup milk
1 tsp soy sauce
¼ tsp pepper
6-8 round rye bread buttered on both sides.

In a large skillet cook onion rings in butter for 10-15 minutes. Arrange onions in greased 12 x 7 ½ inch baking dish. Cover with remaining ingredients. Save some cheese to sprinkle on top. Bake till cheese is melted. 350 degrees, about ½ hour.

Grandma's Best Recipes

Swedish Meat Balls
2 pounds ground beef
¾ pound fresh ground pork
2 ½ slices bread
¾ cup milk
2 eggs
1 onion chopped fine
¼ tsp allspice
½ tsp sage
½ tsp nutmeg
½ tsp pepper
1 ½ tsp salt

Baked Beans (Selma Anderson)
¾ cup catsup
1 pound beans
1 cup bean juice
½ cup molasses
3 handfuls of brown sugar
1 tbsp. mustard
Salt pork or bacon and onion can be used

Cook beans for one hour then use the bean juice or water and put in the rest of the ingredients and salt pork or bacon and bake in 350 degree oven until tender, be sure to put in enough water to cover the beans.

Grandma's Best Recipes

Potato Balls
6 medium potatoes – cook with jackets
Rice the potatoes
1 cup hot milk
Mix in salt, flour and 2 eggs. Stiff enough to form balls. Put a crouton in the center of each one. Have salted water boiling. Drop in water. Boil three minutes. Either beef or pork roast and gravy is good with this.

Calico Beans
1 can pork and beans
1 can kidney beans, drained
1 can lima beans, drained

Brown ½ pound bacon (drain), ½ pound ground beef, 1 cup more or less of onion. Combine ½ cup catsup, 1 tsp dry mustard and 2/3 cup brown sugar. Mix above in casserole 350 degrees 50-60 minutes.

Spinach Dish
1 15-oz spinach
4 eggs beaten
1 cup milk
1 cup shredded Swiss cheese
1 cup cubed firm white bread
½ cup sliced green onion
¼ cup grated Parmesan cheese

Drain spinach and squeeze out all excess liquid. Combine all ingredients and pour into 1 quart baking dish. Cover and bake at 375 degrees for 25-30 minutes or until it tests done.

Grandma's Best Recipes

Theresa's Cold Creamed Cucumbers – Theresa Seabloom
4-5 medium cleaned and sliced cucumbers
1 medium onion
1/3 cup sour cream
2/3 cup mayonnaise
2 tbsp. vinegar
3 tbsp. sugar
Salt and pepper to taste

Fruit Bowl
2 cups water
1 ½ cup sugar
3 tbsp. anise seed
½ tsp salt
Cook 15 minutes. Cool and strain. Pour over fruit and refrigerate – stirring frequently.
Fruit:
Small pineapple
Small honeydew melon
Small cantaloupe
2 oranges
2 nectarines or apricots
2 purple plums
1 cup seedless green grapes
1 lime slice

Grandma's Best Recipes

Macaroni and Cheese
Sauté:
1 large onion chopped fine
1 stick butter
--
12 eggs (beaten)
Cook 16 oz. elbow macaroni till just done and drain.
1 ½ pound medium cheddar cheese grated.

Mix all ingredients well. Bake in oiled pan until eggs are set and cheese is melted. Bake 350 for 40-50 minutes. Cool to room temperature cut in squares and serve as finger food. You can refrigerate and later heat up.

Escalloped Corn
½ cup finely chopped green onion
¼ cup oleo or butter
1 can cream style corn
1 cup whole kernel corn (drained)
1 ½ cup cracker crumbs (36 crackers)
3 eggs slightly beaten
1 cup milk
1 tsp salt
Heat oven to 325 degrees.

Cook and stir green onions in butter in small skillet over low heat until tender. Mix remaining ingredients. Stir in onions. Bake in 1 ½ quart casserole. Bake uncovered till firm. 1 hour 15 minutes.

Grandma's Best Recipes

Stuffed Mushrooms – Sarah Seabloom Rodefeld
1 8oz. package button mushrooms
6-8 strips of thinly sliced bacon
1 medium onion
2-3 ounces of cream cheese (1/3 reduced fat works best)
Parmesan cheese
1 - 1 ½ cups finely shredded cheddar cheese
½ tsp salt – optional

Remove stems from caps and set aside. Place caps in medium baking dish or pie plate with the bottom side facing up. Set aside.

Dice the onion and stems into fine pieces and set aside.

Chop the bacon into small pieces and fry until almost crispy. Add mushroom and onions and fry until onions become clear. Add salt to the mix.

Place bacon mix in a medium sized bowl and add 2-3 ounces of cream cheese. The cream cheese is just meant to hold the mixture together so start with two ounces and add extra as needed. Mix well. Add ¼ cup of cheddar cheese and sprinkle Parmesan cheese over the top. Mix well. (Note: If using regular cream cheese, soften it first. It will make mixing easier.)

Spoon the mixture into each cap of the mushroom. Top each mushroom with the remaining cheddar cheese and sprinkle parmesan cheese over the top. Add ¼ cup water to the baking dish.

Bake 15-20 minutes at 375 or until the cheese is lightly browned.

Substitution: Breakfast sausage cooked as you would ground beef can also be used in place of the bacon.

Grandma's Best Recipes

Tomato Basil Soup – Sarah Seabloom Rodefeld
5-6 pounds of tomatoes
1 large onion
3 TBSP minced garlic
2-3 TBSP dried Basil
½ cup Parmesan cheese
2 rounded tablespoons chicken stock or base
4 ounces heavy cream
2-3 cups water
4-5 TBSP Olive Oil
Salad Croutons

Start by chopping the tomatoes up into medium sized chunks. If you don't like texture to a soup, you can blanche the tomatoes to remove the skins first. Set aside.

Dice the onion into small pieces. Add olive oil, onions and minced garlic to a large stock pot and fry until onions are clear. Add tomatoes, water and chicken stock/base to the onion mixture. Over medium to medium high heat, bring the mixture to a boil.

Using a meat chopper or a potato masher, mash the tomatoes and cook until the mixture begins to turn orange. Remove from heat and add the basil, cream and Parmesan Cheese. Mix well. Let cool for 5-10 minutes.

With an immersion blender (I've used other kinds of blenders/choppers but the immersion blender works by far the best and is the safest when working with hot soup), blend the mixture until it's smooth – 2-3 minutes.

Let sit a few minutes to thicken and ladle into bowls. Top with salad croutons and sprinkle with Parmesan Cheese. I freeze extras to enjoy during the winter months.

Grandma's Best Recipes

Stuffed Jalapeños – Sarah Seabloom Rodefeld
8-10 large jalapenos – more can be used if they are smaller
1 Roll breakfast sausage
2-3 ounces of Cream Cheese (1/3 Reduced Fat works best)
1 - 1½ cups finely shredded Cheddar Cheese
Parmesan Cheese
½ cup water

Using gloves, slice peppers in half the long way and remove seeds. Place in a medium-sized baking dish or pie plate and set aside.

Fry sausage as you would ground beef. Remove from pan and place into a medium sized mixing bowl. Add 2 oz. cream cheese, ½ cup shredded cheddar cheese, sprinkle with Parmesan cheese and mix well. If the mixture does not hold together, add more cream cheese. The cream cheese is meant to keep the sausage together.

Fill the halves with the sausage mixture. Top with remaining cheddar cheese, sprinkle with Parmesan cheese. Add ½ cup water to the baking dish. Bake at 375 for 15-20 minutes or until cheddar cheese is browed.

Let cool for 5 minutes before serving.

Grandma's Best Recipes

A Quick Note From The Chef

The saying "Necessity is the mother of invention" couldn't be more true when it comes to gardening. When I have a successful garden, I'm blessed with an overabundance of veggies – mostly tomatoes and jalapeño peppers.

After weeks of our regular tomato recipes and sharing with all our friends, I had to get creative so things wouldn't go to waste so I came up with a few new recipes.

A friend of mine shared her stuffed jalapeño recipe at a local neighborhood party. It was so good that I had to make it. She gave me the recipe and by the time I got home, I realized I already lost it so I came up with my own version – with a touch of Wisconsin – EXTRA cheese. And, as with my Grandmothers, I found myself adding a pinch of this and a scoop of that, topped with a dollop of something else.

And did I write any of my recipes down? Of course not. So, as I started to get requests for these recipes, I had to try to put those measurements that I so eagerly wanted as I was learning to cook into writing. Now I know why my Grandmothers gave me that look. A dollop is a dollop, a pinch is a pinch. Go forth and cook! I'll spare you that and do my best with those measurements.

Grandma's Best Recipes

And that food shall be for store to the land against the seven years of famine, which shall be in the land of Egypt; that the land perish not through the famine.

Genesis 41:36 The Holy Bible, King James Version

Grandma's Best Recipes

Main Dishes

Grandma's Best Recipes

And he gathered up all the food of the seven years, which were in the land of Egypt, and laid up the food in the cities: the food of the field, which was round about every city, laid he up in the same.

Genesis 41:48 The Holy Bible, King James Version

Grandma's Best Recipes

Main Dishes

Wifenpoof
Peel and slice potatoes. Brown ground beef and onions. Add salt and pepper. Put layer of potatoes, then layer of browned meat, layer of potatoes, etc. On top put one or two cans of tomato soup according to the amount of mixture. Bake 375 degrees for one hour.

Cuban Black Beans with Rice
1 tbsp. olive oil or oil
½ cup chopped green bell pepper
½ cup chopped onion
1 minced garlic clove
1 15 oz. can black beans, drained and rinsed
1 14 ½ or 16 oz. can whole tomatoes, undrained and cut up
½ pound cooked ham, coarsely chopped
½ tsp dried oregano leaves
1/8 tsp ground red pepper (cayenne)
1 bay leaf
2 cups hot cooked rice

Heat oil in large skillet over medium-high heat. Add green pepper, onion and garlic. Cook and stir until crisp-tender. Stir in beans, tomatoes, ham, oregano, ground red pepper and bay leaf. Simmer 10 minutes. Remove bay leaf. Serve bean mixture over rice. 4 servings.

Grandma's Best Recipes

Chili
Brown two pounds of ground beef and 2 large diced up onions. Add 1 large can tomatoes and 1 medium can tomatoes. Add three cans kidney beans. Season with chili powder, salt and pepper to taste.

Rock Cornish Hens
Clean birds. Salt and Pepper. Brush with melted butter. Place in shallow pan. Bake 400 degrees – 40 minutes. During last 15 minutes brush on glaze.

Red Currant Glaze
1 tbsp. butter
½ cup red currant jelly
2 tbsp. lemon juice
1 tbsp. cornstarch
½ cup red wine vinegar
1 tsp salt
3 whole cloves
Cook five minutes.

Baked Chopped Suey
1 pound ground beef – browned
1 cup celery chopped fine
2 small onions chopped fine
1 can cream of chicken soup
1 can mushroom soup
1 ½ cup water
½ cup raw rice
4 tbsp. soy sauce

Put together. Bake in buttered dish for ½ hour at 350 degrees. Put one can chop suey noodles on top. Bake another half hour.

Grandma's Best Recipes

Chili Con Carne (Violet Anderson)
One pound ground beef
1 onion chopped
1 can mixed vegetables
1 box tater tots
1 can cream of chicken soup
1 can milk

Brown beef and onions. Place in baking dish. Add remaining ingredients and top with frozen tater tots. Bake at 350 degrees for one hour or until tater tots are brown and crusty.

No Brown, No Peek Five Hour Stew
2 pounds cubed beef round steak
3 tbsp. tapioca
1 ½ tsp salt
1 medium can tomatoes
1 cup chopped celery
6 carrots, cut up
3-4 potatoes
2 small onions in chunks
1 crushed bay leaf (Optional)
Green Pepper (Optional)
1 slice bread optional
1 tbsp. Worcestershire Sauce

Mix together in a covered pan. Bake at 250 degrees for 5 hours. Do not peek!

Grandma's Best Recipes

Spaghetti (Violet Anderson)
½ cup onion
¼ cup celery
¼ cup green pepper
1 tbsp. sugar
½ tsp chili powder
1 pound ground beef
1 can kidney beans
1 can tomato sauce
1 can tomato paste
1 can tomatoes
Salt and Pepper to taste.

Put onions, celery, green pepper in fry pan. Cook until soft then put ground beef in fry pan and brown. Then add kidney beans and the rest of the ingredients. Serve over pasta.

Danish Chicken
1 package dried beef
Chicken breasts
1 can mushroom soup
1 can cream of chicken soup

De-bone chicken and roll in beef. Put in casserole. Pour chicken soup over chicken then the mushroom soup. Bake at 225 degrees four hours.

Fried Chicken
2 tbsp. instant chicken bullion broth powder
1 cup flour
1 cup bread crumbs
1 tsp paprika
2 tbsp. lemon peel
1 tsp Accent seasoning

Wine Spiced Duck
1 cup white wine or broth
1 clove garlic, crushed
1 tsp thyme
1 tsp oregano
1 tsp seasoned salt
1 tsp pepper
¼ cup oil or melted butter
2 duck breasts
Bacon strips

Combine first seven ingredients. Pour over duck breasts. Refrigerate for 2-3 days. Place marinade and breasts in saucepan. Cover and simmer for 2 hours or until tender and adding water if necessary. Place breasts on broiler rack. Top with bacon strips. Broil for 3-5 minutes.

Chicken Noodle Dish (Selma Anderson)
1 can mushroom soup
½ cup sour cream
Cubed chicken
Onion
Noodles

Brown the onions and mix together with the other ingredients and bake in a casserole dish.

Grandma's Best Recipes

Prue's Dill Fish Bake – Prue Bloom Johnson
4 tbsp. butter
¾ cup sour cream
¼ - ½ tsp dill weed
¼ tsp. seasoning salt

Pat fillets to dry them and place them in a medium baking dish. Pour mixture over fillets, cover and bake at 350 for 20 minutes. Remove cover and bake an additional 10-15 minutes.

This recipe works well with thicker fillets of fish – Salmon, Halibut, Striped Bass, etc.

Dolly's Corned Beef
4 pounds corned beef (you may use the kind that has the spices already in the package, or you may buy plain corned beef and add pickling spices)
2 or 3 pork hocks
1 to 2 cups sherry
3-5 carrots cut into large pieces
6 small parsnips cut into large pieces (optional)
6 medium onions, quartered
1 to 2 cabbages cut into wedges
Salt and pepper to taste

Note: If you don't use parsnips or turnips, then use extra carrots, onions and potatoes.

Grandma's Best Recipes

Potato Pancakes
3 cups grated potatoes
2 eggs well beaten
1 ½ tbsp. flour
1/8 tsp baking powder
1 tsp salt
½ tsp onion juice

Pare large potatoes and cover with cold water. Let stand. Pour off water and grate potatoes. Drain well. Add eggs and mix lightly. Stir in remaining ingredients. Drop from tbsp. onto hot well-greased skillet and brown on both sides. 12 pancakes.

Minnesota Lobster
3 quarts water
1 medium onion
3 pieces celery, cut up
Salt to taste
Northern pike fillets, cut up

Place water, onion, celery and salt in a large saucepan. Bring to a boil. Add fish (frozen or thawed) and boil 5-8 minutes. Drain. Place on a cookie sheet. Put a drop of Tabasco sauce on each piece of fish and brush with butter. Sprinkle with paprika. Place in broiler for 2-3 minutes. Serve with melted butter.

Grandma's Best Recipes

Forgotten Chicken
Sauté 1 pound mushrooms in butter.
Pour into 3-quart casserole dish: Two cans cream of chicken soup & ½ can milk

Add mushrooms. Spread over soup and lightly stir in 1 cup uncooked rice. Place 4 chicken breasts over rice. Sprinkle ½ envelope of dry onion soup mix on top. Cover and bake on 350 degrees for 2 hours.
Don't peek!

Chicken Casserole
1 small box minute rice (1 cup regular rice)
1 can cream of celery soup
1 can cream of mushroom soup
½ can milk or one small can
1 envelope dry onion soup mix
1 frying chicken (cut into serving size pieces)

Grease a 9x13 baking dish or small roaster. Sprinkle minute rice on bottom of pan. Heat the 2 cans of soup with milk, stirring until well blended. Pour over rice and stir until well mixed. Lay piece of chicken over rice mixture. Sprinkle with dry onion soup mix. Seal pan with foil. Bake at 350 degrees for 2 hours.

Chuck Roast In Wine (Great Aunt Lorraine)
1 chuck roast
Garlic salt and ground black pepper
Cut carrots for 5
Five large potatoes cut into quarter size
¼ cup red wine
1 package of Onion Lipton Soup mix
½ cup of water

Place chuck roast in roasting pan, season with Garlic salt and pepper, place cut carrots and cut potatoes around base of chuck roast, add the Lipton onion soup mix and then the wine, pouring over roast—finally add water, enough to cover the potatoes and carrots, bake covered at 350 until done, remove roast and potatoes and carrots and make gravy on stove top with juices by adding a tablespoon of flour to a cup of water and pouring into remaining juices, season to taste (if necessary) and stir until gravy reaches desired thickness.

Grandma's Best Recipes

Savory Spaghetti Casserole
3 tbsp. butter
1 large onion diced
1 green pepper diced
1 ½ pounds ground beef
1 tsp salt
¾ tsp pepper
½ cup chopped stuffed olives
¾ cups catsup
1 cup tomato juice
2 tsp sugar
1 tbsp. Worcestershire sauce
½ pounds spaghetti –cooked in boiling water
½ cup cut mushrooms
½ pound cheese diced

Cook spaghetti in salted boiling water. Rinse well with hot water. Sauté onion and green pepper in butter. Add meat and brown. Mix catsup, tomato juice, sugar, Worcestershire sauce and add to meat mixture cooking until well blended. Mix cooked spaghetti, mushrooms, cheese and olives together. Place ½ spaghetti mixture in buttered casserole. Cover with ½ of meat mixture alternating with spaghetti and meat. Place in preheated oven. Bake 350 degrees at 40 minutes.

Grandma's Best Recipes

Salmon Loaf
1 tbsp. melted butter
1 tbsp. finely chopped onion
2 cups milk
1 ¼ cup finely crushed cracker crumbs
1 tsp salt
1/8 tsp pepper
1 can (1 pound) salmon drained and bones removed
3 eggs beaten
Preheat oven (temperature not given)

Combine butter and onion. Sauté until golden brown. Add milk and heat until lukewarm. Add cracker crumbs, salt and pepper. Blend well. Add salmon to milk mixture, then add eggs. Pour into 9x5 pan. Bake 55-60 minutes.

Swedish Meat Balls
2 pounds ground beef
¾ pound fresh pork
2 ½ slices bread
¾ cup milk
2 eggs
1 onion
¼ tsp all spice
½ tsp sage
½ tsp nutmeg
½ tsp pepper
1 ½ tsp salt

Grandma's Best Recipes

Impossible Cheeseburger Pie
1 pound ground beef
1 ½ cup chopped onion
½ tsp salt
¼ tsp pepper
1 ½ cups milk
¾ cup Bisquick baking mix
3 eggs
2 sliced tomatoes
1 cup shredded cheddar cheese or processed American cheese

Heat oven to 400 degrees. Grease 10 x 1 ½ pie plate. Brown ground beef. Drain grease. Stir in salt and pepper. Spread in pie plate. Beat milk, Bisquick mix and eggs on high until smooth in blender for 15 seconds or with hand beater for one minute. Pour into pie plate. Bake 25 minutes. Top with tomatoes and sprinkle with cheese. Bake 6-8 minutes longer.

Corn Beef Casserole
1 can corned beef chopped up
½ lb. Kraft cheese cubed
1 large onion chopped fine
6 to 8 oz. wide noodles boiled in salt water
1 can cream of chicken soup
1 cup milk, mix with soup

Mix all together. Melt oleo and brown three slices of bread cut into cubes. Stir into casserole. Bake 350 degrees for 40-60 minutes.

Grandma's Best Recipes

One Pan Polish Kielbasa Meal
1 Kielbasa cut into 2 inch pieces
4 medium potatoes, cubed
1 medium onion
½ green pepper (optional)
4 tbsp. oleo

Combine all ingredients in heavy skillet with cover. Over low heat simmer until potatoes are tender. Stir every ten minutes for about ½ hour.

Easy Oven Round Steak
2 ½ pounds round steak
1 package Lipton onion soup mix
½ pint sour cream
1 small can cut up mushrooms, drained
Use a 13x9 cake pan. Cut steak in 1-inch cubes - put into pan. Sprinkle with one package Lipton soup mix on steak. Mix sour cream and water. Pour over steak. Sprinkle mushrooms on top. Cover well with aluminum foil. Bake at 350 degrees for 2 hours. Can be served in casserole with mashed potatoes or baked potatoes at same time. Serves 6-8

Bar B-Ques
2 tbsp. brown sugar
2 tbsp. vinegar
4 tbsp. lemon juice
1 small catsup
1 onion chopped
½ cup celery or celery seed
3 tbsp. Worcestershire Sauce
½ tsp mustard
1 cup water
Salt and pepper

Grandma's Best Recipes

Apricot Chicken
Chicken
Apricot nectar
Onion soup mix

Use breasts and thighs. Place chicken in baking dish. The amount of apricot nectar depends on how much chicken is used. Mix onion soup mix and nectar. Pour over chicken and bake at 350 degrees for one hour. Have enough broth to cover chicken.

Bar-B-Que Hamburgers for Buns
1 pound ground beef
½ cup chopped onion
¼ cup chopped green pepper
¼ cup chopped celery
1 cup tomato sauce or tomato soup
¼ cup catsup
1 tbsp. vinegar
1 tbsp. sugar
1 ½ tsp salt
1/8 tsp pepper

Brown meat and add vegetables and cook until vegetables are soft. Add remaining ingredients. Simmer about 20 minutes. Serve hot on hamburger buns. Enough filling for 18 buns.

Grandma's Best Recipes

Baked Fish with Sour Cream – Jeano Seabloom
2 ½ or 3 pounds fish
Strips of bacon
Oil or butter
Salt and pepper
Onion flakes
1 cup sour cream
½ cup Parmesan cheese
1/3 cup buttered bread crumbs or 4 crushed soda crackers
2 or 3 tbsp. lemon juice

Have fish cleaned and well scaled. Rub inside and out with salt and pepper, oil or butter. Lay it on several strips of bacon or salt pork in the bottom of an oblong baking dish. Make a mixture of the cream, onion, cheese, crumbs and lemon juice and spread over fish. Bake in a moderate oven (350 degrees) until tender. The sour cream browns lightly but stays on top of the fish.

Tuna Fish Hot Dish (Violet Anderson)
1 can tuna fish
1 7oz box shell macaroni
1 can mushroom soup
½ cup milk
1 small onion
1 small jar pimento
Cook macaroni and blanche. Then mix the rest of the ingredients and bake in about 375-degree oven.

Grandma's Best Recipes

Manicotti
½ cup ground beef
1 clove garlic, crushed
1 can creamed cottage cheese
½ tsp salt
½ cup Hellmann's Mayonnaise
8 manicotti shells cooked and drained
1 jar 16 oz. spaghetti sauce
½ tsp dried oregano leaves
Parmesan cheese

Brown beef and garlic. Drain fat. Mix next four ingredients in bowl. Stir in beef. Fill each manicotti with about ¼ cup cheese-meat filling. Place in baking dish. Cover with sauce. Sprinkle with oregano and cheese. Cover with foil. Bake in 350-degree oven for 15 minutes. Remove foil bake ten minutes longer serves four.

Pork Steak Casserole
2 pounds pork steak cubed
1 cup hot water
1 8 oz. package medium noodles cooked
1 cup corn nibblets
1 cup chicken soup or broth
1 cup cream of mushroom soup
1 green pepper finely cut
1 cup finely chopped celery
½ tsp salt
¼ tsp pepper
Buttered crumbs

Brown pork steak - add hot water and cooked noodles. Stir in remaining ingredients except crumbs. Pour into baking dish and sprinkle with crumbs. Bake at 350 degrees for one hour.

Grandma's Best Recipes

Swiss Broccoli Casserole
2 packages 10 oz. each frozen broccoli spears cooked and drained
1 can condensed cream of celery soup
2/3 cup milk
1 can 3 oz. Durkee Real French Fried Onions
½ cup shredded Swiss cheese

Combine soup and milk. Arrange broccoli in an 8x12 baking dish. Put ½ cup French Fried Onions, soup mixture and cheese over broccoli. Bake 350 degrees for 25 minutes. Top with remaining onions. Bake five minutes longer.

Home-style Chicken and Biscuit Dumplings
1 Reynolds Oven Cooking Bag – Large size
2 tbsp. flour
1 package chicken gravy mix
¼ tsp garlic powder
1 ½ cups water
4 medium onions sliced
2 stalks celery sliced
6-8 chicken drumsticks
Seasoned salt and pepper
1 can refrigerated buttermilk biscuits

Preheat oven to 350 degrees. Shake flour in Reynolds Oven Cooking Bag. Place in 13x9x2 baking pan. Add gravy mix garlic powder and water. Squeeze bag to blend ingredients. Place carrots and celery in bag in even layer. Sprinkle chicken with seasoning; place on top of vegetables. Arrange biscuits around chicken. Close bag with nylon tie; Cut six half-inch slits in top. Bake until chicken is tender. 50-55 minutes. Makes 3-4 servings.

Grandma's Best Recipes

Souper Chuck Roast
3-4 pound blade chuck roast
1 package dry onion soup mix
1 can cream of mushroom soup

Preheat oven to 350 degrees. Place meat on large piece of heavy-duty tin foil in roasting pan. Sprinkle with onion soup mix. Top with mushroom soup. Close foil in tent-like fashion to allow for air flow. Roast 2 ½ - 3 hours.

Beef Louise
2 pounds round steak cut into one-inch cubes
1 can cream of mushroom soups
1 package dried onion soup
2/3 cup red cooking wine
1 4 oz. can mushroom stems and pieces

Place meat cubes in a casserole dish. Mix other ingredients. Pour over beef. Cover tightly with foil. Bake at 350 degrees if a metal pan is used or 325 degrees for a glass pan for 3 hours. Serve with rice or noodles or mashed potatoes.

Grandma's Best Recipes

Haluchky
3 or 4 potatoes
1 egg
1 tsp salt
2 cups flour (if too stiff, add ¼ cup or less of water)
1 can sour kraut
2-3 tbsp. butter

Grate potatoes. Mix with flour, egg, and salt. Bring water to a boil in large kettle. Put mixture on board and flatten it a bit. With a knife, cut off small pieces of the batter and drop them into boiling water. Boil until the little dumplings come to the top. Drain and rinse them with cold water. Rinse sauerkraut at least once. Brown the butter and mix with the noodles. Add Sauerkraut. Mix well and salt to taste. This also works well with fried cabbage.

Enchilada Casserole – Sarah Rodefeld
1 to 1 ½ pounds hamburger meat
½ cup diced onion
2 cans enchilada sauce
1 can cream of mushroom soup
8 oz. cheddar cheese

Brown ground been and onion and drain. Tear corn tortillas into small pieces. Mix soup, sour cream, and enchilada sauce in with enchiladas and ground beef and onion. Bake at 400 degrees in lightly greased medium sized baking dish until cheese is melted and sides are bubbly.

Parmesan Panko Fried Fish - Sarah Seabloom Rodefeld
3/4 cup plain Panko Bread Crumbs
3/4 cup Parmesan Cheese
1 tsp Garlic Salt (more less can be added to taste)
4-6 egg whites

This works best on thinner fillets like crappie, bass or thinly cut striped bass or catfish. Mix Panko crumbs, parmesan cheese and garlic salt in wide bowl and set aside. In separate medium sized bowl, beat eggs whites until bubbly and frothy.

Dip each fillet into the egg white and roll in batter until completely covered. We like a super crispy batter so we re-dip the fish in the egg white and roll again in bread crumb mixture. Fry in hot grease until dark golden brown.

Variation #1:
To spice the batter up, mix a tablespoon of Cajun seasoning (this can be adjusted to taste) into the Panko bread crumbs in lieu of the Parmesan cheese. Mix well and fry until dark golden brown.

Variation #2
The parmesan Panko batter can also be used on vegetable such as sliced zucchini or squash. Slice either vegetable thin, roll in olive oil, dip both sides into batter mixture pressing firmly to ensure batter sticks. Place on a foil lined pan sprayed with cooking spray. Bake 8 minutes at 450 degrees. Flip vegetable over and bake an additional 8-10 minutes. Let cool 5 minutes and serve plain or with ranch dressing.

Grandma's Best Recipes

Miscellaneous

Grandma's Best Recipes

And Joseph saw his brethren, and he knew them, but made himself strange unto them, and spake roughly unto them; and he said unto them, Whence come ye? And they said, From the land of Canaan to buy food.

Genesis 42:7 The Holy Bible, King James Version

Miscellaneous

Orpha Pickles
7 cups sliced cucumbers (8 good sized cucumbers)
2 cups sugar
1 cup vinegar
1 green pepper chopped
1 onion sliced

Put together and mix. Add one tbsp. salt, 1 tsp celery seed. Store in jar in refrigerator. Ready in 24 hours. Will keep a long time.

Beet Jelly
10-12 beets. Wash well. Stick beets. Cover with water and cook until done. Strain juice through cloth.
Bring to boil:
6 cups juice
2 packages Sure Jell
½ cup lemon juice
Add:
8 cups sugar
1 small package raspberry Jell-O
Cook six minutes – add pinch of salt and put in glasses.

Grandma's Best Recipes

Chokecherry Syrup
4 cups sugar
½ cup lemon juice
½ pkg. powdered pectin

Mix and boil all ingredients for two minutes. Ladle into jars. Seal and process jars ten minutes in boiling water bath. Excellent on pancakes, waffles and French toast and as an ice cream topping.

Zucchini Jam
6 cups Zucchini, peeled and seeded
6 cups sugar
½ cup lemon juice
1 cup crushed pineapple with own juice
6 oz. pkg. orange Jell-O
1 pkg. Sure Jell

Drain zucchini well. Boil till clear – about ten minutes. Add sugar, lemon juice, pineapple and Sure Jell. Boil another six minutes – Remove from heat – add Jell-O. Stir until dissolved. Pour into sterilized glasses and seal.

Grandma's Best Recipes

Cranberry Slush
2 cups **Christmas** vodka
2 cups cranberry juice cocktail
12 oz. orange juice
12 oz. lemonade concentrate
1 pkg. cherry Jell-O – 3oz
1 cup boiling water
3 cups cold water

Dissolve Jell-O in boiling water. Add remaining ingredients. Mix and freeze. Add to 7 up or sour mix to taste.

Apple Butter (spiced)
16 cups thick apple pulp
1 cup vinegar
8 cups sugar
4 tsp cinnamon

Core and slice apples but do not peel. Add only enough water to cook apples until soft. Press through fine sieve and measure. Combine all ingredients. Cook until mixture remains in a smooth mass when boiling. This will require about 1 ½ hours of boiling. Stir frequently. Pour into sterilized jars.

Dressing for Veggie Salad
1 cup mayo
½ cup French dressing
½ cup sour cream
¼ cup sugar
1 tbsp. vinegar
1 tsp salt
chill

Grandma's Best Recipes

Rhubarb Jam
5 cups Rhubarb
4 cups sugar
Set overnight

Boil 10 minutes in the morning. Add 1 ½ boxes of strawberry Jell-O. Cool.

Soft Pretzels
1 pkg. dry yeast
1 1/3 cups warm water
1 tbsp. sugar
½ tsp salt
3 ½ to 4 cups flour
1 egg beaten
1 tbsp. water
2 tbsp. coarse salt or
2 tbsp. cinnamon and sugar or
1 package onion soup mix

Grease two cookie sheets. Dissolve yeast in the warm water. Stir in the sugar, salt and enough flour to make the dough sticky. Place dough on floured board and knead, adding as much flour as needed to make the dough soft. Divide into 12. Make each piece into a 15 inch rope. Make ropes into pretzel shapes. Place three inches apart on the cookie sheets. Mix the beaten egg and 1 tbsp. water. Brush over pretzels. Sprinkle on salt, cinnamon/sugar or dry onion soup mix. Bake at 425 degrees for 15-20 minutes.

Grandma's Best Recipes

Strawberry Jam
1 quart of berries
1 ½ cups sugar

Boil 5 minutes, then add 1 ½ cups more of sugar and boil 10 more

Blackberry Jelly – Sarah Rodefeld
For the Juice:
4 cups blackberries
4 cups water (or enough to cover the berries)

To make the jelly:
3 ¾ cup blackberry Juice
4 ½ cups sugar (set aside and have ready)
1 box Sure Jell

Place berries in large pot. Over medium high heat, cook berries for 10 minutes mashing them as they cook. Cover a large bowl with a flour sack towel and pour berry mixture into the towel. Using Silicon baking mitts, squeeze juice through the towel back into the bowl. Measure 3 ¾ cups juice and pour into a large stock pan. The large size is important because when it cooks, it will bubble up. Stirring constantly, add sure jell to the mixture and bring to a full rolling boil.

Stirring constantly, add sugar and bring back to a rolling boil. Boil for exactly one minute or until jelly comes to 212 degrees.

Remove from heat. Skim bubbles from top and ladle into sterilized half pint jars. Wipe rims, add lids and bands and boil in a water bath for five minutes.

After 4-6 hours, test lids to make sure there is a good seal.

Grandma's Best Recipes

Sand Plum/Wild Plum Jelly – Sarah Rodefeld
To get the juice:
5 pounds plums
4 cups water

Place plums and water into large kettle. Heat until just boiling making sure not to get it to too hard of a boil. Mash plums with a potato masher until mixture is thick and pulpy. Drain mixture through a colander to get juice mix. Strain the hot juice through a flour sack towel to remove all pulp. You will also need silicone baking mitts to squeeze the juice out and to prevent getting burned.

The Jelly Mixture:
5 cups strained plum juice
1 box Sure Jell
7 cups sugar (have this measured and ready to go)

Bring the plum juice and Sure Jell to rolling boil over medium high heat, stirring constantly. While still stirring, add the sugar and bring to a rapid boil over medium high heat. Cook 2-3 minutes or until temperature reaches 212 degrees.

Remove froth glaze from top of hot jelly and ladle into sterilized ½ pint jars. Boil in a water bath for 5 minutes. Remove from burner and let jars sit it water for five minutes and then remove. Check jars 3-4 hours after to ensure all have sealed. If not, store those in refrigerator and use first. Makes 6-8 half pints.

Grandma's Best Recipes

Pickled Fish
1. Cut fish into small pieces
2. Soak in salt brine for 24 hours (salt brine 1 ¼ cups canning salt to 3 quarts water – enough water to float a raw egg).
3. Remove from brine and soak in white vinegar for 24 hours (enough to cover all fish).
4. Pour off vinegar - pack in jars with slice of onions between layers. A red pepper or chili pepper - not a fresh pepper). Cover with brine:
    a. 2 cups white vinegar
    b. 1 cup water
    c. 1 cup sugar
    d. 2 tbsp. pickling spices

Boil a-d for two minutes, cool. Add 4 oz. white port wine and pour over the fish. Full flavor in one week.

Dressing for Crab Salad
1 cup miracle whip
¾ tsp yellow mustard
¾ tsp sugar
¼ cup dill pickle juice
Salt and pepper to taste
Milk
Garlic powder
Lettuce, tomatoes, onions, celery and cucumbers.

Taco Dip
Mix 1 8oz. package cream cheese and taco flavoring to taste with 2-3 tbsp. of sour cream. Spread on bottom of dish or cookie sheet. Sprinkle shredded cheese and lettuce on top. Top with diced tomatoes and onions. Canned jalapeño peppers or black olives can also be added.

Grandma's Best Recipes

Cocktail Wieners
½ cup prepared mustard
1 cup currant jelly
1 package of cocktail wieners (Little Smokies)

Melt jelly and mustard together in saucepan. Add wieners to mixture and heat.

California Oil Dressing
½ cup Wesson Oil
½ cup sugar
1/3 cup catsup
¼ cup vinegar
Juice of one lemon
Dash of red pepper
Dash of salt
1 tbsp. onion juice or finely chopped onions

Shake well and keep in a sealed jar in the refrigerator.

Thousand Island Dressing
2 tbsp. green pepper
1 hard-boiled egg
1 tsp Worcestershire sauce
1 tbsp. catsup
1 cup mayonnaise
2 tbsp. chili sauce

Sweet and Sour Dressing
½ cup salad oil
¼ cup vinegar
½ cup sugar
¼ cup catsup
2 tbsp. Worcestershire sauce
For spinach salad – Spinach, sliced egg, and anything else you like.

Grandma's Best Recipes

Blender Hollandaise Sauce
3 egg yolks
1 tbsp. lemon juice
½ tsp salt
2 drops Tabasco sauce
½ cup melted butter

In blender, mix all ingredients except butter. Slowly pour in butter while mixing on low speed. Refrigerate if not using immediately.

Hot Bacon Dressing (for spinach salad)
½ pound bacon diced
¾ cup diced onion
½ cup white vinegar
½ cup red wine vinegar
1 tbsp. sugar
1 cup beef broth
3 tsp cornstarch
1/8 tsp pepper
½ cup bacon fat

Sauté bacon until crisp. Drain and set aside. Sauté onion in bacon drippings. Add vinegar, pepper and sugar. Dissolve cornstarch in beef broth and add until slightly thickened. Pour over well washed spinach and sprinkle with bacon pieces and serve. Use more broth or sugar according to taste.

Grandma's Best Recipes

Marinade for Roasting Pig – From Cuba
1 quart lemon juice
1 pint orange juice (frozen)
1 pint grapefruit juice (frozen)
½ can oregano
½ can cumin
¼ can black pepper
4 tbsp. salt
2 small lime juice
6 bulbs crushed garlic

Bailey's Irish Cream
4 eggs
1 14 oz. can sweetened condensed milk (Eagle Brand)
1 ½ cups blended whiskey
½ tsp instant coffee
½ tsp coconut extract
1 tbsp. chocolate syrup
1 tsp vanilla
1/8 tsp almond extract

Put in blender and beat for 2 minutes. Pour in bottle and refrigerate. Makes 1 quart.

Grandma's Best Recipes

Sausage Recipe
2 pounds ground beef or pork or venison
1 cup water
1 ½ tsp. liquid smoke
1/8 tsp garlic powder or more if you want
½ tsp onion powder or more if you want
½ tsp mustard seed
2-3 tbsp. curing salt (Morton's Tender Quick)
1 tbsp. sugar

Mix all above ingredients except meat. Let stand 20 minutes. Add meat. Mix with hands. Roll in 2 rolls. Wrap in aluminum foil shiny side towards meat. Refrigerate 24 hours. Punch holes in foil with paring knife. Put on rack in a pan. Bake 325 degrees for 1 ½ hours.

Onion Rings
4 large Bermuda onions
3 cups unsifted flour
2 tsp salt
1 ½ tsp baking powder
3 eggs
2 ¼ cup milk
3 tbsp. salad oil
3 – 4 cups dry bread crumbs

Peel onions. Cut and separate. Heat oil to 375 degrees. Sift flour with 2 tsp salt and baking powder. Set aside. Beat eggs slightly. Stir in milk and 3 tbsp. oil. Add flour mixture and stir until smooth. Dip rings in batter and let excess drip off and then roll in bread crumbs. Fry in deep fat until golden brown.

Grandma's Best Recipes

Fruit Punch
2 liters 7-Up
1 small frozen orange juice
1 small frozen lemon juice
Mix and chill.

Baked Onions
4 large sweet onions
2 tbsp. butter
2 cups (8 oz.) shredded Swiss cheese
1 can cream of chicken soup
Mix in ½ cup milk
1 tsp soy sauce
¼ tsp pepper
6-8 round rye bread pieces buttered on both sides

In a large skillet cook onion rings in butter for 10-15 minutes. Arrange onions in a greased 12x7 ½ baking dish. Cover with remaining ingredients. Save some cheese to sprinkle on top. Bake until all cheese is melted good. Bake 350 degrees for about ½ hour.

Wild Rice Dressing
1 cup wild rice
¼ cup bacon
¼ cup chopped celery
2 medium onions
1 tsp salt
¼ tsp pepper
1 cup mushroom soup
1 cup mushrooms

Soak rice ½ hour in 4 ½ cups water and chicken bouillon cubes. Cook one hour. Fry bacon crisp. Sauté onion and celery. Add soup, mushrooms and rice. Bake 1 hour.

Grandma's Best Recipes

Pizza Sauce
6 ounces or 2/3 cup tomato paste
½ cup water
1 tsp salt
1tsp oregano
Dash of pepper

Lutfisk (Ling) – Christmas Special for Grandma Selma
Soaking of Swedish Lutfisk
To every 2 ½ lbs. dried spring ling:
½ pound slake lime
½ pound soda
Water

To get fish ready for Christmas Eve, begin December 9th. Divide fish in 2 or 3 pieces and put in wooden tub. Add cold water to cover and place in cool place, changing water every day for four days. Then scrub fish on both sides and remove. Empty tub. Cover bottom with lime; arrange layer of fish, skin side down, on top. Cover with lime, add another layer of fish, skin side up, and cover with lime. Dissolve soda in a little warm water; add cold water. Pour slowly over fish until very well covered. Solution should always cover all of fish. Last of all, put light press over tub (board with large stone on top). Soak fish 5-7 days or until soft enough to let finger penetrate thickest part easily. Remove. Rinse tub, return fish and cover with fresh cold water. Change water every day first three days, later twice every week. Fish is ready to cook after 4-6 days in fresh water. Cook small piece to test. Fish may be kept in water a long time but becomes hard if kept too long.

Grandma's Best Recipes

Boiled Lutfisk (Ling)
3 pounds soaked lutfisk (see recipe above, pg. 126)
Salt
Water

Skin and cut up fish. Place pieces close together in cheesecloth and sprinkle with salt. Place on fish rack. Bring very slowly to boiling point and simmer 10-15 minutes. When ready, drain and remove to hot platter. Always serve with salt, black and white pepper, mustard, boiled potatoes, melted butter and white sauce. Lutfisk can also be served with green peas.

Fried Fresh Smelts
2 ¼ pounds fresh sardines or smelts
½ tablespoon salt
Bread crumbs or rye or whole wheat flour
To Fry:
3 tablespoons butter
Clean fish removing heads. Rinse well under cold running water and drain. Salt and dip in bread crumbs or flour, then fry in butter until nicely brown on both sides and serve with mashed potatoes.

Oyster Cracker Snack
2 packages oyster crackers
2 packages Hidden Valley Original Ranch Style salad dressing
Mix:
½ tsp garlic powder
½ tsp lemon pepper
½ tsp dill week

Mix altogether in large bowl with cover and shake and shake some more. Mix 1 cup Crisco oil and shake and shake some more. Then eat.

Grandma's Best Recipes

Glazed Nuts
2 cups sugar
1 cup light corn syrup
½ cup water
1 tbsp. angostura bitters
1 cup butter
3 cups assorted shelled nuts
1 tsp soda

Combine sugar, syrup and water in large saucepan. Add bitters and butter and boil till 300 degrees. Heat nuts into 250 degrees – about 15 minutes. Stir nuts and soda into syrup. Stir quickly to blend. Divide mixture equally between two well-buttered 15x10x1 inch pans. Using two greased forks, spread out nuts into a single layer. Cool. Break into pieces and store in an airtight container in cool dry place. Yield 2 ½ pounds glazed nuts.

Peppy Almonds
3 cups almonds (do not toast them)
In a 9x13 pan melt and mix:
1/3 cup oleo
1 tsp Lawry's season salt
1 tsp chili powder

Add almonds and mix well with a pancake turner. Place in 300-degree oven for 30 minutes. Be sure to turn them every 5-10 minutes. When done put pan in refrigerator until cold then turn out on wax paper and dry for one day. Store in covered can.

Grandma's Best Recipes

Chex Party Mix
½ cup butter or margarine
1 ¼ tsp seasoned salt (2 tsp)
4 ½ tsp Worcestershire Sauce
2 cups corn Chex cereal
2 cups rice Chex
2 cups bran Chex
2 cups wheat Chex
1 cup salted mixed nuts

Preheat oven to 250 degrees. Heat butter in large shallow roasting pan in oven until melted. Remove and stir in seasoned salt and Worcestershire sauce. Add Chex mix and nuts. Mix until all pieces are coated. Heat in oven for one hour. Stir every 15 minutes. Spread on absorbent paper to cool. Makes 9 cups.

Pickled Eggs
12-16 eggs – Simmer 10-15 minutes
1 ½ cup vinegar
½ cup water
1 tsp salt
1 tsp pickling spices
3 tbsp. sugar
Let stand two days

Pickled Eggs (Jeano Seabloom)
1 quart vinegar
2 cup water
3 tsp salt
3 tsp sugar
3 tsp pickling spices
1 onion

Cook five minutes – pour over eggs when hot.

Grandma's Best Recipes

Pickled Mushrooms
2/3 cup Heinz White Vinegar
½ cup salad oil
1 medium clove garlic – minced
1 tsp sugar
1 ½ tsp salt
Dash ground pepper
2 tsp water
Dash Tabasco sauce
1 medium onion sliced and separated into rings and 12 ounces mushrooms – refrigerate. It's ready in 3-4 days.

Dressing for Coleslaw
¼ cup cider vinegar
1 cup mayonnaise dressing
2 tbsp. granulated sugar
Wisk above until well blended
Add to finely shredded cabbage and carrots.

Barbecue Sauce
½ cup honey
½ cup soy sauce
2 cloves crushed garlic
2 tbsp. catsup
½ cup water or wine
Put together in a sauce pan and heat. Spoon over ribs. Bake sauce and ribs for 1 ½ hour until done. Baste periodically.

Dressing for Three Bean Salad
½ cup sugar
¼ - ½ cup vinegar
¼ cup oil
Salt
Celery seed

Grandma's Best Recipes

French Dressing
1 cup sugar
1 cup Mazola oil
1 cup catsup
½ cup vinegar
1 medium onion chopped fine
Dash Worcestershire sauce
1 clove garlic
Mix oil. Add catsup, mix. Add vinegar, etc.

Salad Dressing
About 1 cup Miracle Whip
½ tsp yellow mustard
1 rounded tsp sugar
Shake – garlic powder
½ tsp pepper
Dill pickle juice
Add little milk to right consistency.

Celery Seed Dressing
1 cup oil
1 tsp salt
1 tsp mustard
7 tsp sugar
Medium onion, grated
½ cup vinegar
1 tbsp. celery seed
Blend.

Grandma's Best Recipes

Baked Dill Pickles
3 quarts water
1 cup canning salt
1 quart cider vinegar

Bring brine to a boil then cool. Pack dill sized cucumbers tightly in jars with plenty of dill and a small onion. Pour cold brine over and seal tight. Put jars in cake pan with two inches of water. Bake at 250 degrees for 1 hour in preheated oven.

After Dinner Coffee
1 tsp cappuccino coffee in wine glass
1 tsp brown sugar
1 oz. Amaretto
Fill glasses with hot water
1 tbsp. whipping cream

Russian Tea
2 cups tang
1 pkg. Wyler's lemonade
¾ cup instant tea
½ cups cloves
1 tsp cinnamon
¼ cup sugar

Mix dry and store. When used put 1 tsp to 1 tbsp. to taste per cup of hot or cold water. Liquor can be added (Vodka)

Grandma's Best Recipes

Homemade BBQ Sauce – Sarah Rodefeld
3 14-oz bottles of ketchup
5 tbsp. liquid smoke
6 tsp. chili powder
1 ½ cups sugar
1 tsp cayenne pepper (more or less to taste)

Mix together and pour back into ketchup bottles or into pint canning jars. If using ketchup bottles, an extra bottle will be needed.

Orange Delight Drink
1 6-ounce can frozen orange juice
1 cup water
½ cup sugar
1 tsp vanilla
9-10 ice cubes
1 cup milk

Combine all ingredients in blender. Cover and blend 30 seconds. Serve right away.

Grasshopper (Drink)
¾ ounce fresh cream
1 ounce Cream de Cacao
1 ounce green Cream de menthe

Shake with cracked ice or mix in an electric blender. Strain into glass.

Grandma's Best Recipes

Homemade Clay
2 cups flour
1 cup salt
1 tbsp. powdered alum
Water
Food coloring or poster paint

Mix with about 1/3 cup water or as much as needed to make the mixture pliable. If clay isn't colored it becomes dirty looking from use. It will keep indefinitely if it is wrapped in a damp cloth and in a covered container.

Play-Doh
4 cups flour
2 cups salt
8 tsp cream of tartar
4 tbsp. baby oil
4 cups water
Food coloring

Mix well and cook medium heat until it forms a ball.

Russian Tea
2 cups tang
1 pkg. Wyler's lemonade
¾ cup instant tea
½ cups cloves
1 tsp cinnamon
¼ cup sugar

Mix dry and store. When used put 1 tsp to 1 tbsp. to taste per cup of hot or cold water. Liquor can be added (Vodka)

Grandma's Best Recipes

Orange Fizzy Drink (Great Aunt Lorraine)
3 two liter bottles of 7up, and 1.5 quart size carton of orange sherbet

Combine all ingredients in a large punch bowl, whip carefully with an egg beater, and then serve immediately .in party sized cups Serve right away

Green grasshopper Fizzy Drink (Great Aunt Lorraine)
3 two liter bottles of 7up, and 1.5 quart size carton of lime sherbet

Combine all ingredients in a large punch bowl, whip carefully with an egg beater, and then serve immediately .in party sized cups. Serve right away.

For even more fun--make ***Over The Rainbow Fizzy Drink***

Just substitute in rainbow sherbet!

Grandma's Best Recipes

Soups

Grandma's Best Recipes

And they said unto him, Nay, my lord, but to buy food are thy servants come.

Genesis 42:10 The Holy Bible, King James Version

Grandma's Best Recipes

Soups

Aunt Janice's Cabbage Soup
Brown 1½ lbs. of ground sirloin, drain
Add ½ cup chopped celery
Add 1 cup chopped onion, 8 cups water, one medium head cabbage

Bring to boil, reduce heat, simmer 10 minute

Add 1tsp. beef bouillon, 1½ tsp. salt, 1 tsp. pepper
Simmer 10 minutes.

Add two 15 ounce cans of tomato sauce
Simmer 10 minutes

Add 1 tbsp brown sugar and ¼ cup of ketchup
Simmer 10 minutes and then serve.

Dill Pickle Soup
5 dill pickles
4 tsp butter
1 quart water
1 chopped carrot
1 potato cubed
Chopped celery
Parsley
½ cup sour cream
Chopped dill or ½ cup pickle juice

Sauté pickles in butter. Bring the rest to a boil and cook until vegetables are done. Add sour cream and sautéed pickles and dill.

Grandma's Best Recipes

Potato Dumplings
3 cups mashed potatoes
1 cup bread crumbs
2 eggs
1 tsp salt
1 cup flour (may want to add another ¼ cup)

Mix together with cold hands. Form into small balls. Cook in boiling water uncovered for 30 minutes. Serve with pork roast and sauerkraut. It is best to use mashed potatoes that have been made the day before.

Easy Crockpot Potato Soup
1 30oz bag diced hash browns (square chunks not shredded)
32 oz. chicken broth (I use Chicken stock for richer flavor)
1 can cream of chicken soup
1 package cream cheese
1 cup shredded cheddar cheese
½ cup diced onions
1 tsp garlic powder
1-2 cups fried diced/cubed ham

Cook on low for 8 hours. Stir occasionally.

Hamburger Soup – Recipe
½ pound hamburger (ground chuck)
1 package onion soup mix
15 oz. can stewed tomatoes
8 oz. tomato sauce
8 oz. water
1 package frozen mixed vegetables, Dash oregano

Simmer 45 minutes.

Grandma's Best Recipes

Egg Drop Soup
4 cups chicken broth
3 eggs beaten
3 small scallions or green onions chopped

Bring broth to a boil. Remove from heat. Slowly pour beaten eggs into soup stirring constantly. Stir in scallions or green onions. Serve immediately. Makes one quart.

Onion Potato Soup
6 slice bacon
4 medium onions (2 cups sliced)
2 large potatoes pared and diced (2 ¼ cups)
1 13 ¾ oz. can of chicken broth
½ cup water
1 tsp salt
1 14oz can evaporated milk
2 tbsp. fresh parsley

In large saucepan, cook bacon until crisp. Reserve 2 tbsp. of drippings. Drain and crumble. Cook onions in drippings until tender, not brown. Add diced potatoes, broth, water and salt. Cook 10 minutes till tender. Mash potatoes slightly. Stir in milk, parsley and bacon and heat. Serves 6.

Grandma's Best Recipes

Dumplings
1 cup sifted flour
2 tsp baking powder
½ tsp salt
½ cup milk
2 tbsp. cooking oil
2 tbsp. snipped parsley

Stir just to moisten, drop from tablespoons into boiling stock. Reduce heat and simmer 12-15 minutes. 6-8 servings.

French Onion Soup
2 medium onions, thinly sliced
2 tbsp. butter or oleo
2 cans beef broth
1 – 1 ½ can water
1 tsp Worcestershire sauce
4 slices French bread or croutons
Grated Parmesan cheese
4 slices mozzarella cheese halved or shredded

Place onions and oleo in 3-quart casserole dish. Cover. Microwave on high 8-10 minutes or until onions are tender. Add beef broth, water and Worcestershire Sauce. Microwave covered on high for 5-7 minutes or until mixture boils. Toast French bread. Place on paper towels or plastic tray – sprinkle with Parmesan cheese. Top with mozzarella cheese. Microwave on high 15-30 seconds or until cheese is melted. Place one slice of bread in each serving bowls. Pour soup mixture over bread. 4 servings.

Grandma's Best Recipes

Hearty Potato Soup
5 cups sliced potatoes
3 cups boiling water
½ tsp salt
6 slices bacon
3 cups sliced onions
2 cups milk
¼ tsp pepper

Cook potatoes in boiling salted water until tender. Drain. Reserve water. Mash potatoes. Cut bacon into ½ inch pieces and fry until crisp. Add onions and cook until golden brown. Combine bacon, onions, potatoes, water and mashed potatoes. Add milk and pepper. Heat and serve. Serves 6.

Fish Chowder
Clean and skin fish. Put into boiling water and boil until tender enough to pick meat off the bones. Remove from water and save water. Add the following to water and boil until vegetables are tender:
½ cup carrots
½ cup onion
½ cup celery
½ cup potatoes

When vegetables are tender, add the de-boned fish, 4 tbsp. butter, ½ cup milk, and salt and pepper to taste. Most fish can be used, bluegills etc.

Grandma's Best Recipes

Flemish Stew
Sauté 2 medium onions sliced in 2 tbsp. oil
3 pounds beef, cubed and browed with onions
Add:
1 10 ½ ounce can beef broth
2 cans mushrooms
1 can beer
1 clove garlic
1 ¾ tsp salt
¼ tsp pepper
¼ tsp thyme
1 bay leaf

Bake in 350-degree oven for two hours. Thicken with cornstarch or flour. Serve over noodles.

Broccoli Soup
1 scant cups flour
3 sticks butter or butter substitute
1 quart chicken broth
1 medium onion diced
1 clove garlic diced fine
3 stalks celery diced
Pinch of thyme
2 bundles broccoli peeled and diced (Cauliflower can be used instead of broccoli)
One quart hot milk
Salt to taste

Melt butter or butter substitute. Add onion and garlic. Sauté until clear. Add celery and sauté until slightly soft. Add thyme. Stir in flower. Cook ten minutes. Add chicken broth. Stir until smooth. Add broccoli. Add milk and season with salt. Makes 2 ½ quarts. (I steam broccoli and leave in chunks before adding)

Grandma's Best Recipes

Black Bean Soup (Sopa de Frijoles Negro)
Cook beans until soft
Add two onions
3 tsp vinegar
3 tsp wine
Some pimento
Camine
Salt pk.

Or - en Espanol
Sopa de frijoles Negro
Cook in water until soft blandito
Add cebollo
Ajo
3 cucharita vinegar
3 cucharita vino seo
Pe quito pimiento
Camino tambien
       Purico de sol   (I *did my best to read the Spanish*)

Grandma's Best Recipes

Leftover Turkey Soup (Great Aunt Lorraine)
Turkey carcass (left over from turkey)
3 stalks of celery, chopped
4 carrots cut into small pieces (as you prefer
1 large onion, chopped
Salt, garlic salt and pepper
One package of dry egg noodles

Place turkey carcass in large pot, cover with water, season with salt, garlic and pepper, and bring to boil. Then lower heat to simmer. Simmer until meat falls from carcass, remove carcass, add celery, carrots and chopped onion. Bring to a boil again, and then reduce to simmer until added ingredients are cooked. Prepare egg noodles separately according to package instructions, drain egg noodles and add to broth. Serve.

Grandma Florence's Soup Noodles/Dumplings – Florence Bloom
2 eggs, beaten
½ tsp. salt
2/3 to ¾ cup flour

Knead until dough holds its texture (stretchier than cookie dough). Roll out and cut into 1/8 inch strips. Cook in broth – simmer ½ hour. I use this recipe for dumplings. Instead of rolling, I place small chunks of dough into boiling chicken soup and cook for 5-10 minutes.

Grandma's Best Recipes

Seabloom Family Mealtime Prayers

Come Lord Jesus, be our Guest;
And let these gifts to us be blest.
May our souls by Thee be fed
Ever on the Living Bread.
Amen. Public Domain

Father, bless the food we take,
And bless us all for Jesus' sake.
Amen. Anonymus

God bless not only food and drink
But what we do and what we think
And grant for all our work and play,
That we may love Thee more each day.
Amen. Author Unknown

For all Thy goodness and Thy grace,
O Lord, to Thee be thanks and praise.
Amen   author unknown

God is great and God is good,
And we thank Him for this food.
By His hand we all are fed;
Give us, Lord, our Daily Bread.
Amen Public Domain

Be not forgetful to entertain strangers: for thereby some have entertained angels unawares.
- Hebrews 13:2, The Holy Bible, King James version

O give thanks unto the LORD; for *he is* good: for his mercy *endureth* for ever.
- Psalm 136-1, The Holy Bible, King James version

Grandma's Best Recipes

About The Author

Like all the Anderson girls, Sarah grew up in the small northern Wisconsin town of Rhinelander. Unlike most young girls who were into dresses and more feminine things, Sarah was a country girl at heart and spent her free time roaming the family's land located in Pine Lake on the shores of Thunder Lake. Al and Jeano had their hands full just keeping track of her. From raking turtles out of the lake at ice out, to cooling off in mud puddles in the summer, to collecting salamanders in the fall, she and her three dogs were always on the go. After Jeano's untimely death when Sarah was 10 years old, she spent more time with her grandparents after school and during the summer months, learning the old fashioned ways of cooking, cleaning and life in general. Art and Dorothy were full of stories about the family in their younger days. Some of her favorite stories were of the horses that the Seabloom family had both in the United States and during their time in Cuba. She would always admire Art's old Cuban saddle in the basement.

Like many young girls, her love of horses grew stronger and stronger. Al finally broke down and got Sarah a horse of her very own, a horse named Amber. And, as the best gift ever possible, Art gave her that Cuban saddle in the basement. Like a car, Amber gave Sarah more mobility and an avenue to broaden her local travels and the ability to enjoy the great outdoors even more.

During the summer when she wasn't busy with her horse, Sarah would spend hours with Dorothy and Art at the family resort. Since she could walk, Art played a huge role in teaching Sarah how to fish. From a cane pole, to a casting rod, and finally to the fly rod, Art was a patient teacher; and he shared his lifetime of fishing secrets with her! She and Art would spend many summer evenings out fishing until dark, often coming in with grandiose fish tales to make everyone laugh and wonder. When Sarah was young, Jeano had been an avid photographer and had many photos that Sarah loved to look at, so it was only natural that in high school, Sarah took a photography class and instantly fell in love. Al had kept Jeano's camera, and when the time

Grandma's Best Recipes

came, he gave Sarah the camera after he saw the same love in her for photography that Jeano had.

That very camera provided the framework for her ongoing life-long love love of photography!

After Sarah graduated from high school, she was off to college. On her first summer break, her friend set her up on a blind date with a co- worker of whom, at one point, she was not too fond; but then, after 20 questions, and solid reassurance that he had gown on her from the year before (and that he was really great) Sarah went on the date. One date led to another; and a year after her first date with Nels, they were married.

College brought them south to Nels' home town of Madison. Nels graduated the following year, and he and Sarah made the long move to Arkansas for his first job. After a year there, Nels was offered his dream job in Oklahoma, and they made the move to Oklahoma.

Nels is also an avid fisherman and hunter, and he enjoys the great outdoors as much as Sarah. Fishing and hunting play a key role in their lives and has from day one. From fishing in the spring and summer, and hunting in the fall and early winter, there isn't much they don't do outside.

After searching for years for the right place to live, fish, hunt and enjoy life, they found their dream home in Maud, America. Country life has allowed Sarah to enjoy her photo passion and provides the chance to hunt and fish and enjoy country living every day. Once their day jobs are done, they spend evenings and weekends working cattle, roaming the farm with their dogs, and enjoying life to the fullest – including cooking whatever tastes good – and usually recipes from Grandma's recipe collection! And these recipes are not only Grandma's best recipes, as you will see, they are the favorite recipes of Sarah's entire extended family!

www.ingramcontent.com/pod-product-compliance
Lightning Source LLC
LaVergne TN
LVHW021942060526
838200LV00042B/1900